10 e

ALSO BY DAVID HARRIS

The Last Stand

The League

Dreams Die Hard

The Last Scam

I Shoulda Been Home Yesterday

Goliath

OUR WAR

OUR WAR

WHAT WE DID IN VIETNAM
AND WHAT IT DID TO US

DAVID HARRIS

TIMES T BOOKS

RANDOM HOUSE

Copyright © 1996 by David Harris

All rights reserved under International and Pan-American Copyright Conventions. Published in the United States by Times Books, a division of Random House, Inc., New York, and simultaneously in Canada by Random House of Canada Limited, Toronto.

Library of Congress Cataloging-in-Publication data is available.
ISBN 0-8129-2576-9

Random House website address: http://www.randomhouse.com/

Printed in the United States of America on acid-free paper

98765432

First Edition

for Cheri

ACKNOWLEDGMENTS

A number of people helped me sort through the thoughts and remembrances upon which this book is built, either through their own work or in conversation or both. I wish to thank them all: Kathy Robbins, Kate Paley, John Sullivan, Lacey Fosburgh, Sophie Harris, Peter Schwartz, Nancy Ramsey, Rusty Schweikart, Rick Baum, Sim Van der Ryn, Ruth Friend, Franz Schurman, Andrew Lam, John Keker, Jonas Honnick, Jack McCloskey, Neil Reichline, Layton Borkan, Patrick Hallinan, Susan Sward, Loren Hallinan, Bill Bertain, Fred Branfman, Fred Goff, Rodney Gage, Kit Bricca, Joe Maizlish, Ray Correo, Ron Kovic, Scott Camil, Elaine Harris, Nguyen Thai, Thich Hai Thong, and the Data Center.

I owe a special acknowledgment to my editor, Steve Wasserman, whose craft and insight were invaluable and without whom this book would never have been written.

OUR WAR

1

——

L IKE A LOT of us, I took the war personally in
those days.

And I still do. I lived molded to the war's
shape for so long that, indeed, my person has
retained the war's bend in ways both petty and profound. I was a boy when it began and a man when it
finally came to an end. It echoes in me to this day: when
pacing nervously, I walk a nine-foot oval, as though I
were still confined in my cell in maximum security;
when I attend a black-tie affair, there is still part of me
that looks around the room and flinches, convinced
that if these people had any idea who I really am, I
would be sent packing; when the Pledge of Allegiance
is recited, I still take a deep breath and ask myself if
I really want to repeat it along with everybody else.

I remember the war as someone it obsessed and imprisoned. And, while it no longer preys on my mind, it is still a subject about which I find it difficult to summon disinterest or distance. I have never known the war at arm's length. I remember it on my skin and in my bones; I remember it as a weight in the pit of my stomach and I remember it as a pain in my chest, late at night and alone.

Much has passed under my personal bridge since the war ended, and, as I have weathered further episodes of loss and helplessness, my heart has opened enough to reexamine long-standing wounds. Now fifty years old, I have come to yearn for something far more than remembrance.

What I seek is a Reckoning.

I first experienced the posture I have in mind in an intensive-care ward some three years ago, when Lacey, my wife of nineteen years, hopelessly comatose, was removed from artificial life supports. Then I held her as she died, a casualty of a desperate failed struggle with breast cancer. I knew her better than anyone, and I could tell from the calm in her heart as she passed that while she'd waited in unconsciousness, attached to a breathing machine, she had somehow taken responsibility for her life and prepared herself to leave it. I had read fictional and religious descriptions of such reckonings, in which lives are revisited in a summary accounting, and Lacey's last moments seemed to confirm them.

Reckoning has been a word full of meaning for me ever since. Coming to terms with ourselves is what we do when we reckon, and reckon with our war is what we must do: stand outside our fears, revisit what we did so many years ago, and clear our souls of this perpetual shadow.

Our reckoning is not to be engaged in lightly or with less than the whole of our selves. At the very least, I expect that taking a good look at the war will be a painful and demanding process. Hard things need to be said, often in hard ways. And, as raw as my memory of the war is, I still do not come easily to that task. I am not a hard man. Quite the contrary. I am usually eager to get along, am reluctant to express personal disapproval, and tend to swallow my complaints in the normal course of life. I like to please and put people at ease. But there are subjects about which there is no easiness, and this war is one of them. I cannot avoid its ugliness, nor do I think such avoidance useful.

So also with my anger. Some of it, too, is unavoidable, even necessary, though again I am not, on the whole, an angry man. Few have ever seen my temper, and while I make a point of speaking my mind, I mostly shy from enlarging confrontations, and in this instance I worry that my surviving outrage will sound bitter so many years after the fact. But I am outraged still. And I mean to say things that bother me deeply and that I know will disturb others, as unfortunate as that disturbance may be. And I hope others will do likewise until we finally run out of things to say.

Last Thanksgiving I was back in Fresno, California, where I grew up, at my mom's house. I told her that I was writing, once again, about the war. She said she hoped that the country could put all that stuff that happened over Vietnam behind us now, that we needed to move on. I told her that was not exactly what I had in mind.

We need to face up to it first. For me, this is not just about us and not just about now. It is an engagement in the sacred human ritual of studying our own tracks, an attempt at the consecration of those who have gone before through the contemplation of how and why their lives were spent. If healing what the war left behind is possible, I look for such healing in this therapy of honest self-examination and informed acceptance. I also find such a process the most fundamental form of respect. It obliges us to value one another's passing and refuse to spend lives without an accounting. So now, so much later, it is finally time to account.

That, of course, is no small piece of work. Our experience in Vietnam is a lot for any of us to take on, especially after having spent much of the last two decades avoiding it as best we could. We should not kid ourselves, however. Holding to our denial will never allow us to escape the war. That avoidance means only that, rather than owning our experience, we will continue to be owned by it.

An extreme example of being owned by our experience is described by the psychiatric diagnosis post-traumatic stress disorder, PTSD, the Vietnam generation's contribution to the study of mental health. The first patients diagnosed with PTSD were trying to grapple with leftovers from Southeast Asian combat. Their battlefield experience had been much too intense to be assimilated on the spot, so it was deferred and deferred until it began to recur spontaneously, usually at the instigation of familiar scenes or sounds: the whip of helicopter blades, backfires that crack like rounds from an AK-47, Caterpillar tracks that rumble and clank like an armored personnel carrier advancing over the red dirt, hard as concrete during those last weeks before the monsoons began. With that trigger, the patient would return to a firefight outside Chu Lai or a bunker near Magic Mountain or a paddy in the Delta or a ridge near the Rockpile, trapped in an endless repetition of the emotions surrounding the original unresolved trauma.

I never quite understood the power of the phenomenon until I was diagnosed with it myself. My PTSD emerged following Lacey's death. Some eight months after I sat with her body, laid out in a Buddhist wake in the front room of our house, I was overwhelmed by a fog of unfocused anxiety that just descended and never left. To extricate myself, I spent the next year sorting out all I had gone through over the three years of illness and treatments before her death, allowing myself to feel all the fear and pain that I had held at bay in the interest of supporting her battle. Slowly, my experience became my own again — terror ebbed out of all my internal nooks and crannies; loss, grief, and panic surfaced where I could become acquainted with them face to face; what had happened to me in real time now happened over and over again on replay, letting me accustom myself to all that had gone on, this time at a speed I could live with.

And so it may be for all of us: our body politic clogged with undigested experience, strung up on the very same dilemmas we never dealt with twenty-five years ago, when the killing was still going on. Our disorder is plain to see: having made lying an accepted government function, our government is now overrun with liars; having made our public posture heartless as a matter of policy, we are now unable to bring our heart to public affairs; having made killing a measure of our national efforts, we watch helplessly as killing has become one of our principal cultural currencies; having failed to look our transgressions straight in the face, we have not been straight with one another since; having refused to live up to our values, we are now increasingly without values; having made language into hype, we now have nothing believable to say. I may just be shell-shocked, but that sounds a lot like PTSD to me.

In truth, that disorder is our nation's running thirty-year metaphor. And our emblem is those poor boys who grew old real quick, came home, and still live with that war every day.

When Lacey and I first set up housekeeping, we lived around the corner from a Veterans Administration hospital that specialized in outpatient psychiatric services. I often crossed paths with the patients at the neighborhood grocery store, where both they and I would stop to buy cigarettes. Occasionally one would bum a smoke off me instead. I got to know Leroy that way. He was at the store a lot. He'd been a Spec 4 with the First Air Cavalry. He liked $1.50 a quart burgundy and smoked Camels. We got so we would banter whenever we encountered each other, every day more or less the same way.

"What's up, Leroy my man?"

"Same old same old."

"Sing me a few bars," I said.

"Jes' like always," Leroy answered. " 'They's somewhere out there in the trees and we's stuck out here in the middle with no motherfuckin' place to hide.' "

I suspect every American who remembers the war knows just how Leroy felt.

Back when the war was still going on, lots of people I knew went to great lengths to find a political theory to explain the discrepancy between who America thought it was and who it acted like. And in that search, isms eventually proliferated, turning the issue to ideology rather than behavior, and making the discussion a lot more complicated and a lot less clear. I kept pace for a while—I was once a Stanford honors student in Social Thought and Institutions—but eventually I lost all tolerance for such theories. I have retained only one in the years since.

We Get What We Do, nothing more. Especially when lives are on the line. We do not get what we mean to do: intention is meaningless. Nor do we get what we tell ourselves we do: appearance counts little and rhetoric even less. We get only the getting, never what we have identified to be got. All means are ends in motion, as ends are means in a static state. Acts that fail to embody their object also fail to realize it. I call this the Do Theory. The war taught it to me.

And, while I am unwilling to give the Do Theory the universal subscription of an ideology, I have consulted it in making decisions throughout my life, to largely positive effect. I have also found it has value in sorting the past. Translated into that tense, of course, the theory reads, We Got What We Did, both a cogent explanation and yet another compelling reason to seek out what happened so many years ago deep in the tall grass and reckon with it once and for all.

And, if the Do Theory is accurate, doing so will prove its own reward.

.   .   .

As I reckon, I have to remind myself that making scapegoats is not the way to proceed. There are indeed those among us more deserving of blame than the rest, and they must be held individually accountable, but the healing we need requires us to look to ourselves before we single anyone out. When we account for this war, we must begin by accounting for it all together. It was, after all, *our* war.

When a nation acts, all its citizens are joined insolubly in responsibility for the consequence of their national behavior, bound to that mutuality for as long as they remember their history, bound generation after generation, carrying its weight as part of their ancestral inheritance. And so it is with us and our war: as far as the fact of it is concerned, as far as all the implications of it having happened at all, as far as carrying the weight of those years and all that carnage, at the bottom line of our enterprise, each of us was the other and vice versa, a single moral organism that must now come to terms together with what we all have done in all of our names. The war's dominant conjugation was first-person plural. We cannot lay it off on any one, any ten, any twenty, or any thirty thousand of us. We cannot exempt our individual selves, whatever we actually did while the war raged. When the question is asked, Who did this? we must all raise our hands.

And in that communion, we eventually redeem ourselves and all those who must follow us and carry their own share of that national shame. And when we have finally declared ourselves, declared ourselves without withholding, with hearts open as though to our loved ones, our anguish will become simply memory and we will heal and grow strong. We were all truly in this together.

Stopping the war once meant everything to me.

I left Stanford University after spending my senior year as student body president, ticketed to graduate with honors, winner of the Poetry Prize, and I gave up all thoughts of career and graduate school and lived out of my 1961 Rambler, traveling up and down the Pacific coast, searching for others who meant to throw their bodies on the cogs of the machine. I delivered at least a thousand speeches while America cut its swath through Southeast Asia. I spoke in auditoriums and on street corners, and in every speech I ever gave I said the war was a crime against everything America was meant to be and urged any young man called to the draft to join me and refuse to go. Each such specific call to disobedience was technically a felony violation of the Selective Service Act, worth a maximum of five years in prison. After I accumulated some five thousand years' worth of such potential violations, I stopped counting. Nor did I bother to calculate what I had coming for all the occasions when I called on soldiers to join us and refuse their orders as well. As long as the war was the law, I wanted to be an outlaw.

That, of course, meant I was watched by the FBI and military intelligence, interrogated at length, and arrested four times in ten years for acts of civil disobedience—all misdemeanors except for one felony violation of the Selective Service Act, charging me with refusing to go to the war when my name was called. For the felony, I spent twenty months of my life "in the custody of the Attorney General of the United States," most of it shuttling between a maximum-security cellblock in a federal correctional institution on the Texas–New Mexico border and the punishment cellblock on the floor below. When they let me go, I had a parole officer to whom I reported for another sixteen months while continuing to organize against the war. I didn't stop organizing until the 1973 Paris Agreements formalized American withdrawal from direct combat. I participated in my final demonstration against the war in 1975, just three months before Saigon became Ho Chi Minh City. By then, the war had consumed a decade of my life.

In the darkest days, when just handfuls of us, young and scruffy, seemed to be bearing the brunt of bringing the most powerful nation in the world to its senses, I always believed that when we finally stopped the war, when the troops came home, when the bombing ceased, somehow America would come to a settling of accounts with ourselves, both taking responsibility for the irresponsible and doling out responsibility to those deserving it in larger measures than the rest. And in the process we would fashion a communal assessment of what we did and what doing so meant about us, who we really were, and who we really needed to be. I was young in those days and supposed that history would demand such an assessment and that we would automatically accede.

I'm not young anymore, and I'm glad I didn't hold my breath waiting for that reckoning to arrive.

The closest we've come to it over the intervening decades is an informal consensus among the American body politic that the war was a "mistake." As a social construct, "mistake" was certainly a significant step out of the dispute that had surrounded our war almost since it started: "mistake" allowed the war to be mentioned in polite company with a reasonable chance of avoiding offense. Everybody agreed. The war was certainly a "mistake." Some thought it was a mistake because we never completely leveled Hanoi, some because our strategy amounted to a crime punishable under the Nuremberg precedent, and most, of course, for reasons somewhere in between.

For all of us, "mistake" provided an emotional anonymity and, as such, a refuge from the pain of what we did.

Mistakes happen. They are somehow like the weather, part of life: it is a mistake to buy the wrong size dress, a mistake to leave loose lug nuts on the wheel of an automobile, a mistake to stick your finger in boiling water, a mistake not to check the pockets of your pants before you put them in the washer, a mistake to go camping in August without mosquito repellent, a mistake to wear brown shoes with a black suit, a mistake to invest public funds in exotic financial ventures, a mistake to leave home without making sure the stove is turned off. Mistakes are what the quality control division pulls off the assembly line; mistakes are what the retailer sells out the back door as seconds; mistakes are what the cook doesn't want to let out of the kitchen and the customer will send back if he does. Mistakes earn an ass-chewing from the boss. Mistakes are apologized for or ignored, usually with little consequence. Everybody makes them.

While it may be an accurate conclusion, calling the war a mistake is the functional equivalent of calling water wet or dirt dirty. And it is now long since time that we moved on to an understanding considerably more profound.

Let us not lose sight of what actually happened.

In this particular "mistake," at least 3 million people died, only 58,000 of whom were Americans. These 3 million people died crushed in the mud, riddled with shrapnel, hurled out of helicopters, impaled on sharpened bamboo, obliterated in carpets of explosives dropped from bombers flying so high they could only be heard and never seen; they died reduced to chunks by one or more land mines, finished off by a round through the temple or a bayonet in the throat, consumed by sizzling phosphorus, burned alive with jellied gasoline, strung up by their thumbs, starved in cages, executed after watching their babies die, trapped on the barbed wire calling for their mothers. They died while trying to kill, they died while trying to kill no one, they died heroes, they died villains, they died at random, they died most often when someone who had no idea who they were killed them under the orders of someone who had even less idea than that. Some of the dead were sent home to their families, some were reduced to such indistinguishable pulp that they could not be recovered. All 3 million died in pain, often so intense that death was a relief. They all left someone behind. They all became markers visited by those who needed to remember and not forget. The loss was enormous, and "mistake" is no way to account for it. A course of behavior that kills 3 million people for no good reason cannot be passed off as something for which the generic response is Excuse Me.

We can begin our reckoning by giving the war a different name.

Contrary to the childhood doggerel, names can make a huge difference. They are central to how we identify and perceive. Thus, I have come to prefer the name for the war the Vietnamese use. They call it the American War.

The first time I heard that formulation spoken aloud was with Vinh, a pedicab driver in Ho Chi Minh City. Vinh had been a draftee in the air force of the Republic of Vietnam and spent a brief internment in a reeducation camp after the war ended. Now he practiced his pedicab trade from a corner just down the block from the Saigon cathedral. "The American War" sounded unusual when it came out of his mouth, but it was immediately comfortable to my ear. I did not need to have it explained.

"Of course," I said, "the American War."

"Vietnam War same same?" he asked.

"Same same," I answered. I guess I'd known as much for a long time.

So many Vietnamese died and so much of Vietnam was devastated, but the heart of it all was not really about Vietnam or the Vietnamese. They were just in the intersection when our convertible rolled up.

This war was about us. We made it happen. It was ours.

And, even at this late date, any genuine reckoning on our part must include assuming the full responsibilities of that ownership. Nothing less will do.

2

I N THE OLD DAYS, when I was doing nothing but trying to stop the war, we assumed that, whenever the time finally came that someone who had been through at least some of what we were enduring sat in Lyndon Johnson's chair, things would be different. But by that standard I must say Bill Clinton has been a disappointment. He might have made an enormous contribution to our reckoning, but instead his attitude toward his own past has only added to the murkiness obscuring the realities of our war.

There is, of course, no small irony in Clinton's eventual designation as the most visible member of the antiwar eruption that consumed the nation through the back half of the sixties and into the front half of the

decade after. In fact, he hardly made it into the movement at all, participating in his first and only demonstration against the war more than half a decade after
the Tonkin Gulf Resolution, the official starting point
of our debacle. And that demonstration was in Lon-
don, making it even safer. He was nowhere near the
lead edge. Rather, he was just a student politician
apprenticing for the same role in adulthood, a type
I saw a lot of during the year I was student body
president at Stanford. The South produced more than
a few of them, all looking as if cut from the same
buttoned-down mold and many surprisingly liberal for
that side of the Mason-Dixon line. When it came to
the war, they quoted Senator J. William Fulbright of
Arkansas, who, by 1967, was one of the policy's most
visible opponents in the Senate. They also gave
speeches to people like me about the importance of
staying inside the law and using the political process.
When it came to their personal draft status, they usually milked the system of student and vocational deferments to its maximum and used their connections to
their best advantage.

Certainly that was Clinton's history. He'd been a
junior aide for Fulbright, and the senator let his draft
board back in Arkansas know that Bill was doing
important work in the national interest. Clinton even
scared up a rare last-minute ROTC assignment in his
home state at the time he was most worried that he

might be called to fill one of the perpetual vacancies out where the dying was being done. And he never was. The personal twists were particular to him, but the process and outcome were run of the mill: more than 11 million other Americans picked their way around those orders just like Bill did. The military was never a very popular destination.

Which did not, of course, prevent Bill's draft status from becoming a major issue when he challenged George Bush for the presidency in 1992. So much so that it became offensive. I didn't mind all the questions, I thought they were largely appropriate; what bothered me was that no one was asking the comparable questions of George Bush. Bush sat in Congress while the war raged and voted to send even more soldiers after those who'd already been wasted. And when it came time for his own son to take one of those places out where guns were being fired and black smoke lifted off the napalm patches, the young Bush got a stateside National Guard posting, a privilege that might well have been the difference between life and death at the time it was granted. So how did George justify all that? Since no one asked him, we'll never know. It was just like the old days: the weight of authority was still being accorded to the architects of disaster, and the assumption of disbelief was still being accorded to their opposition. The same old men who demanded that we fight their war and got away with it were now demanding that we justify our failure to do so and were getting away with that, too. Apparently, avoiding conscription might disqualify someone for the presidency but sending American troops out to die for no good reason would not.

That all made Clinton's victory particularly sweet, but most everything since then has been downhill. During his campaign and in the course of his first four years in office, Bill Clinton has been afforded literally hundreds of opportunities to say clearly, "The war was wrong. I didn't think we should be doing what we did, and I wanted no part of it." Instead he has slithered, dithered, mumbled, jumbled, slid, hid, deferred, conferred, allowed, disallowed, invented, and reinvented. To hear Bill Clinton address the subject, you'd think that there was no war he grew up in, that it never posed any dilemmas, that he'd never joined his generation's rebellion, even at the last minute, and that whatever went on in the Vietnam of his youth was no longer of any real consequence to the United States of America.

The crowning irony came in 1995, when, jousting with the Gingrich Congress over spending cuts, Clinton blocked their attempts to eliminate the budget of the military conscription registration office that Jimmy Carter had reinstituted after the Soviet invasion of Afghanistan. In the low-grade dustup that followed, the president's people let it be known that Bill Clinton thought the system was essential to the national defense.

Power insulates those who have it, even from their own history, but the rest of us should remember that the commander in chief felt a whole lot different when his own ass was on the line so many, many years ago.

Perhaps Bill Clinton's greatest disservice to the cause he visited so briefly in his youth has been leaving the unmistakable impression that people spoke up like that in order somehow to avoid the war.

Nothing, of course, could be further from the truth. Speaking up against the war put everyone who did it in deeper than they'd ever been before. Keeping quiet was a much better way to avoid if avoidance was what you had in mind. Speaking up was a defining act: a step out of the safety of anonymity, a step into the hostile glare of generic Americanism, a challenge to the hometown sauce in which we'd been basted all the way to draft age. It was also a clear departure from the acceptable, a declaration of identity outside everything we had once assumed, a mortgage drawn on our future, and a scary line to cross. The import of doing so shook families by their foundations.

We must remember, every arrangement for this war had two categories: the young and everybody else. The young were expected to sacrifice themselves on its behalf, and nothing was expected of everybody else. No manufacturers were ordered to suspend their profits, no consumers were instructed to suspend their consumption, none of the socially established were asked to miss their bank payments or abandon their jobs, football fans weren't forced to turn off their weekly television broadcasts, beer drinkers weren't told to drink less beer, bird watchers weren't informed they had to watch fewer birds, taxpayers were hardly even told to pay more taxes. Only the nation's supply of young adults were issued orders for the war that had to be followed.

In retrospect, it comes as no surprise that the line separating our age group from the others soon ran throughout America. At the time, of course, this division was considered a great sociological mystery. The papers called it "the Generation Gap," and for a while national reporters showed up every couple of weeks to interview us in the hope of writing something profound about this schism. Most of the analysis was recycled tripe, but the schism itself was extraordinarily real. Everyone experienced it, and in truth there was little mystery to it. I suspect cannon fodder have always felt themselves a breed apart.

Every male of draft age — turned eighteen and not yet past twenty-six — indeed had a separate reality.

As casualties began increasing and the Vietnam command began pleading for more troops, draft calls escalated along with everything else. By the middle of

1966, deferments were tightening up, and lots of boys began getting letters from the commander in chief, telling them just when and where to report.

My first notice came several months after I renounced my student deferment. The papers, delivered by registered mail, ordered me to report for my preinduction physical at an address in Fresno in the last week of November 1966. I drove back in my 1942 Oldsmobile. It had been my grandma's car until the year before. Reporting time was 5:30 A.M., when light was just beginning to splay along Fresno's winter streets.

The induction center was in the warehouse district, north of downtown and just east of the railroad tracks. Many of my childhood memories were framed by those tracks and tattooed with the whistle the fruit trains blew as they moved through Fresno in the middle of the night. This morning was cold, with ground fog stacked up in slabs so thick it was impossible to see to the next corner. I was wearing an old war surplus pea coat, and there was a dead dog stiff on the sidewalk down the block from where I parked my Olds.

The induction center looked like just another processing plant, divided into several open, fluorescent-lit spaces, marked by long stretches of linoleum upon which a line had been painted, connecting the various stations of the examination. Those of us who had been called would parade through them, step by step, dressed in our underwear, coughing for the doctor who checked hernias, answering a question or two from the psychiatrist, sitting on the table while our reflexes were checked. The morning would seem interminable, and it would be almost noon by the time the sergeant in charge told us we were done and would hear from the government shortly.

The day began in a room full of desks. I took a seat along with everyone else scheduled for the preinduction physical examination. Most would pass, and all of those who did were pretty much guaranteed to be in boot camp within the next three to six months. A few of those would be in Vietnam in time for the Tet Offensive in January 1968. That morning we slumped in chairs, nursing Styrofoam cups of coffee, as the sign on the pot announced, courtesy of Lyndon Baines Johnson, President of the United States. Unless they already knew each other, no one looked at anybody else head-on. Most just snatched glances sideways and tried to focus nowhere in particular.

There were black kids from the west side of the tracks, Okies from Mendota, Avenal, Dinuba, and the like, lots of Mexicans, a couple Armenians, lots of Fresno white trash, and me. I was the only one with a beard. Most of the Okies already had GI haircuts except the one closest to me, a *pachuco*-looking dude with his hair greased back in wings on either side of his head. When everyone had reported, the sergeant in charge gave each of us a form to fill out. I completed mine first. The *chuco* dude was one of the last to finish. While we waited for the few who trailed him, he made conversation with me. He wanted to know what I did.

I said I was a college student.

"Fresno City College?"

I shook my head.

"Fresno State?"

"No," I said, "Stanford University."

The *chuco* pulled back some, giving me a bewildered look. "What the hell are *you* doing *here*?" he asked.

This was indeed a poor boys' war. Blacks died in it at twice the proportions of whites, Hispanics at three times. The student deferment ensured that. During the war's prime years, not having one was a sure ticket to the rice paddies, so everyone who did have one ought to cross himself tonight when he drives past the cemetery: some boy behind those gates may very well have died in his stead. Which was not, I thought, the way America was supposed to fight its wars.

The workings of the student deferment were simple: its holder was immune from induction while enrolled full-time and making "active progress" toward a degree. Counting everything from community college systems to graduate schools, that student body included the children of most of the great white American middle class, the people whose sons didn't have to go to work after high school and who aspired to the professionalism associated with higher education. In that context, the student deferment was a political free ticket. It had almost single-handedly served to keep "peacetime" conscription palatable for the decade and a half leading up to the war.

The people to whom it spoke were accustomed to hauling the American Dream around on the front seats of their Chevrolets. They, of course, expected no less for their sons. They also were the foundation of any governing majority in America, and each of the war's presidents knew that if the war ever started killing off this constituency wholesale, his political survival would immediately be at issue. So the system stayed the same until the war was on its last legs and largely given up for lost. And as a consequence it was mostly the boys of the poor, the sons of the social edge, the less than fortunate, the oddballs who fell through a crack, those who couldn't afford to go to school full-time, those who worked with their hands or their backs, the lost, the lazy, the penitent, the undercapitalized, the unwanted, the uncouth, the needy, and the fuckoffs who would end up conscripted into the ever-darkening tunnel.

The first decision I ever made about the draft was over the deferment I had coming if I wanted it. In the spring of 1966, the Selective Service System, as the official arm of conscription was known, administered a test that all students seeking deferments had to take. I declined. If Americans fought wars, I had concluded, either everybody should be obliged to fight them or nobody should.

Mine was an extreme minority opinion, needless to say. Just about the only other complaints about the student deferment were from those who didn't have one, and, of course, if those people had mattered, they *would* have had one.

That inequality was only one of many legacies of the Selective Service System. And by no means its worst. That description may be reserved for the war itself. Conscription was its precondition. The war might very well have been impossible if the Selective Service System hadn't already been in place and functioning smoothly. "Peacetime" conscription had been national policy since the year after I was born. We were inured to it. Everybody I knew registered when he turned eighteen and never gave it a second thought until late in the game. The preexisting capacity to conscript was a given, and the purpose to which it was put did not have to seek advance justification in the political marketplace, so planners in Washington could assume unlimited manpower when they made policies. In effect, the Selective Service System was a blank check for instant and undeclared war. When the focus turned to Vietnam, there was no need to convince the nation to pledge its sons: those sons were already pledged; no need to ask permission: permission was long since given; no need to suspend the protections of the Constitution: they were already suspended. Using us was simple. The issue was open and shut before we even knew it was an issue. All that was required was cranking up the dial and turning the machine loose.

What followed was, in many ways, a simple case of easy come, easy go.

Coming out against the war meant having to explain yourself to Mom and Dad, and that was often the hardest part. Everyone went through it, and most cringed at having to do so.

My dad and I ended up in a motel room in Palo Alto on a day in 1967 when he'd driven up to Stanford to visit. By then I'd already refused to accept a student deferment, publicly returned my draft cards to the government, been classified 1-A, and passed a preinduction physical. I had already announced that I would refuse any order to report, and I expected to receive one any day. I also expected the government soon to file conspiracy charges against my organizing. This motel room visit was Dad's final attempt to head me off.

He hadn't come to defend the war. Dad had served every day of World War II with the Army Signal Corps, been discharged as an officer, and attended another twenty years' worth of Army Reserve meetings when I was growing up, but he thought this war was dumb and getting dumber. Typically, however, he mostly kept his opinion to himself and insisted on arguing the contrary whenever we spoke on the subject. His argument that day was about me: I was going to ruin my life. I had enormous possibilities and I was about to sacrifice all of them. He was crying, only the second or third time I'd ever seen his tears. He begged me not to do what I was about to do, and I had never, ever heard him beg.

I felt I owed my dad a lot, but I refused his request. I told him it was my life to ruin, and, while I didn't know just what was going to happen, whatever happened was not going to include cooperating with this war. It was a crime, I told him, and I was never going to be part of it, no matter how many times they sent me to jail. I was crying too by then, and neither of us had much of anything left to say to the other.

Which did not, however, keep him from being my dad. He sat through every day of my trial, frozen in a perpetual grimace. Back in Fresno, he took a lot of cold shoulders at his luncheon club on my account, not to mention a lot of midnight crank calls about his no-good-commie son. When the government moved me to Arizona for a seven-month stopover on my way to Texas, he drove down to visit me every other week or so. He left his law office after work Friday, motored straight through to Arizona, then turned around and drove back in time for the next week's work.

I doubt if my dad had ever even peeked at the insides of the federal prison system until he came to see me. He practiced small-time real estate and inheritance law and never touched criminal cases. And he was straight as an arrow, a man who wouldn't fudge on his taxes no matter how many others did. During his first visit, however, his life turned on its ear. The guards let him through the gate into the visiting yard, and out of nowhere he was seized with an overwhelming urge to attack these people who were holding his son. He'd never felt anything like it in his life. Somewhere inside him a gasket blew, and he had to restrain himself for fear he'd go for one of the hacks' throats.

When he told me about his experience, long after things had become easy between us again, he had a kind of twinkle in his eye and a grin on his lips. He seemed to have enjoyed his trip to the other side of life enormously.

Dad is dead now—he died just a week before Lacey—and when I remember the two of us during the war, I can't help but think that twinkle may well have been the nicest present I ever gave him.

My father, when making his final attempt to beg me into changing my course almost thirty years ago, declared that I would ruin my life by taking on the war the way I was. To him, I was poised on the edge of a void. But Dad turned out to be wrong. I had faith that I could not lose by acting as close to right as I knew how, and, in my eyes at least, my faith has been vindicated. I took my life in my hands, and I have managed to keep my grip on it since. That in itself made it all worthwhile.

When I was beginning my freshman year at Stanford, the hottest intellectual topic of the moment had been framed by the philosopher Hannah Arendt and her book *Eichmann in Jerusalem.* In a discourse centered on what she called the banality of evil within the Nazi organization for Jewish extermination, she posed the question of just what we would be obliged to do if we were Germans faced with this kind of horror, and we freshmen sat around Wilbur Hall trying to answer it. Our war years followed in short order, and I believe my answer passed that test in real life rather than academic speculation: all citizens who live in a state share responsibility for its activities; having been ordered to do something by duly constituted authority absolves no one of anything; evil is not only banal, done by the ordinary in ordinary ways, it is also participatory, and it only happens if everyone does his or her little bit to make it possible. I am proud to say that, when my turn came, I declined to do mine.

I was not one of the war's opponents who was enamored of the other side. I did not tour Hanoi or march with any NLF flags. I made it a point not to root for governments who would not allow me to run a printing press out of my garage if I so chose. These were, after all, believers in a one-party state who had a record of disturbing ruthlessness when dealing with their internal opposition. That said, I found little to distinguish their failings from those of our surrogate, the Republic of Vietnam, and no compelling reasons to make enemies of one and allies of the other. The only profound difference between the two options was that one seemed to have the weight of Vietnamese patriotism behind it while the other seemed to have only us. That the war should end seemed obvious.

We did not, however, stop it. Having spent a decade organizing against the war, I had hoped it would end in an upsurge of revulsion and renunciation of what America had done, but there was no such closure. The war ended by attrition, when it had lost all its value, failed in the polls, sunk without even a blip in the ratings, when we just plain could not stand to have it around anymore. Then, we did what we had to do to get out of it while pretending that we had completed whatever it was we imagined we had set out to do in the first place. And, whatever promises we had made to the contrary, we left without even the intention to look back at the tall grass from which we emerged. Thenceforth, our war was officially Over, written off as mistaken, and, ollie ollie oxen free, no one had to face up to anything that had happened.

Or so we thought.

3

WHEN I ATTEMPT to pin down just when I got my first glimmer that this would be the kind of venture for which so many souls would be held so accountable, I end up back in June 1963. I had just graduated from Fresno High School, where I'd been an honor roll student, football player, debater, and named Boy of the Year. My grandmother was a member of the Daughters of the American Revolution, my father of the Scottish Rite. My older brother would eventually serve as a surgeon with the Eighty-second Airborne Division, and I was still eight months away from mandatory registration for military conscription, waiting for work to start at the produce shed where I would earn enough money packing cantaloupes that summer to pay for my freshman year at Stanford University. In the meantime, I cruised with my buddies in someone's Ford convertible.

One of our destinations that June was the Fresno Municipal Airport, where President John F. Kennedy paid my hometown a twenty-minute visit on his way to dedicate a new federal reservoir seventy miles farther up the San Joaquin Valley. He arrived in a small propeller-driven airplane because the Fresno airport was not yet ready to take one of the new passenger jets like Air Force One. We gathered behind a chain-link fence fifty yards away. The heat lifting off the asphalt was searing, and the pavement blistered. After taxiing back and forth, the president's plane came to a stop, and he stepped out. He was wearing a suit and tie, and we were wearing cut-off Levi's. We cheered. He waved. He would be dead in another five months, the moment his brains splattered all over the trunk of his Lincoln convertible captured forever on a loop of film that would be replayed over and over again for the rest of our lives.

The presage of events even worse came in a wire-service photo I saw in my father's copy of *Time* magazine shortly after my high school graduation. It was taken by a United Press International correspondent at the intersection of Phan Dinh Phung Boulevard and Le Van Duyet Street in downtown Saigon. The

Buddhist monk Thich Quang Duc had doused himself with a combination of gasoline and diesel fuel, ignited the mixture, and was now captured for posterity sitting perfectly erect in a full lotus posture with flame running up his body and leaping off his head in a long, slow curl. Behind him, the old Austin automobile in which he had been driven to the spot was parked with its hood up. Quang Duc's face was set, his eyes were level, his mouth made no cry, he revealed only a hint of the agony of burning alive.

The story accompanying the photo said that the monk had immolated himself to protest the suppression of Buddhism by the government of President Ngo Dinh Diem, the Roman Catholic autocrat supported by the young government of the Roman Catholic John F. Kennedy. Close to twenty thousand American military "advisers" were then deployed in South Vietnam to administer "advice" in Diem's suppression of the growing guerrilla insurgency of the National Liberation Front.

I already knew something about Vietnam. I read *The Fresno Bee* daily, *Time* every week, and *National Geographic* every month. I knew Vietnam was an exotic place, ten thousand miles across the Pacific, divided in two, like a good deal of the world those days. It had been a French colony until the French were defeated at the Battle of Dienbienphu in 1954 by the native forces led by Ho Chi Minh. The issue about

Vietnam as *Time* laid it out was whether or not the place would "go Communist." The Republic of Vietnam, now occupying the southern half of the country, was America's bulwark against that eventuality. Its self-appointed government was led by Ngo Dinh Diem, his brother, and his sister-in-law. Diem and his brother would be dead within six months, executed by South Vietnamese generals acting in collusion with officials of the Kennedy administration.

I assimilated the printed information, of course, but the photograph of the flaming Thich Quang Duc was the story as far as I was concerned. It stayed with me. More than thirty years later I traveled to the Thien Mu Buddhist pagoda on the Perfume River in the city of Hue—near the path along which American troops had to blast their way in order to retake the city after the National Liberation Front's Tet Offensive—to view the Austin in which Thich Quang Duc rode to his immolation. It was maintained as a sacred relic. I was by then something of a part-time Buddhist myself and knew that the monks of Thien Mu were considering more immolations to protest the suppression of Buddhism by the Communist government to whom the authority of Ho Chi Minh and the NLF had devolved. I sat with the abbot and thought often of the Austin while he chanted the pagoda's daily prayers late in the warm afternoon. Afterward, the car came up briefly in our conversation.

"This car," he said, "it is holy, very holy."

I answered that I believed it was.

Back in June of 1963, of course, I didn't believe any such thing. I was just plain riveted. I had a teenager's curiosity about death, and I had never before seen a photograph of someone actually dying. I looked at the photo almost every day, hoping somehow to catch a glimpse of what this monk saw. I could not imagine a more difficult end. Then my mother, unaware of my fascination, threw that issue of *Time* in the trash. By then I knew in my pores that Thich Quang Duc had to have been in an enormous field of white light to endure what he did, erect with his knees folded, unwavering until he toppled over dead, consumed by flame. The magazine treated the monk's suicide as a crank gesture, but some part of me understood already that this was serious business, undertaken only for the most serious of reasons.

As it turned out, the Venerable Thich Quang Duc, already an old man at the time of his immolation, was putting us on notice. A lot of souls, including our own, were hanging in the balance.

The enormity of our ensuing moral disaster can only be reconstructed by calculating the considerable distance that soon grew between who we thought we were and who we ended up acting like. The starting point in any such spiritual measurement is always high school civics, at least for those of us who lived through the war. Everyone took it, and everyone I grew up with believed it.

America was the outpost of democracy. Every citizen was respected, most rights defended, both here and abroad. We appeared on foreign soil only as liberators. Without self-serving agendas, we brought only our democratic values. And we had an obligation to support those who subscribed to them and oppose those who did not. We went halfway around the world to help the deserving, rescue the desperate, and serve the Good and the True. We acted with respect and fellowship, we were loyal and valiant friends. We came to reason with and to support, to defend a way of life from those who would defile or destroy it. We were the world's best hope and, if not completely selfless, at the very least tirelessly benevolent. Fear not, folks, we said, the Americans are coming.

Part of me remains amazed that we swallowed all that, but we did. Somehow such dogma resonated when we were still cruising in Ford convertibles and waving at the president. We were the baby boomers, we watched *Victory at Sea* on TV and passed through puberty when Dwight D. Eisenhower was commander in chief. We were raised on World War II, our fathers' war. It was the Americans who stopped Hitler and Tojo. It was the Americans who stopped the concentration camps. It was the Americans who made sure those guilty of the most heinous of crimes were apprehended and punished. And since the war it was the Americans who had drawn the line against the Stalinist nightmare. We were convinced that everything and everyone we touched was the better for it. God seemed to have given America a blank check.

So we donned the mantle discarded by the French colonialists and propped up a government that no one in Fresno would have tolerated as their own for sixteen seconds. When that government proved much better at taking our money than at winning the hearts and minds of its citizenry, we stepped in to help with the task. We knew little or nothing about the place and referred to the locals informally as gooks, slopes, squints, and dinks. We expected to kick ass, take names, and be home by Christmas. But we weren't, not that Christmas or the next or the next or the next or the next or the next or the next.

Unable to locate our guerrilla adversaries, we uprooted whole villages and evacuated them to bastions surrounded by barbed wire, almost always against their wishes. Since we were in control of both everything and nothing, we measured our success by how many people we were able to kill and announced those statistics on a daily basis. We created free-fire zones where we claimed the right to do anything we wanted to anyone found there without our permission. We burned the homes of people we suspected of helping the other side. We tracked our adversaries with a secret police network of political prisons and assassins. We often killed whoever aroused suspicion and asked no questions. Eventually, we barricaded ourselves in urban forts and attempted to drive the countryside to us. We marked off sections of landscape on the map and sent bombers to saturate the areas in the hope of making them uninhabitable. Before we left, we had dropped some 250 pounds of high explosives for every single human being in that part of the Southeast Asian subcontinent.

We also occasionally raped, pillaged, killed for sport, and transported heroin. The first three crimes were usually spontaneous actions by individual soldiers that went virtually unpunished; the fourth was a de facto government policy. Everywhere we stayed for any length of time, young children scavenged our garbage dumps, old women sold us dime bags of heroin, and impoverished teenagers sold us blow jobs. Within a year of the passage of the Tonkin Gulf Resolution in 1964, opening the way to the war's endless escalation, the growth industry in Saigon was breast enlargements to make bar girls more attractive to boys used to cruising in Ford convertibles.

By the time the war was winding down and Richard Nixon and Henry Kissinger were negotiating our withdrawal with the NLF and North Vietnamese in Paris, our army was in disarray, officers were being assassinated by their men, and the war had been widened to the entirety of Southeast Asia, leading to a similar set of noxious allies and a million or so more dead. Then, finally recognizing that everything we had tried over the last ten years had failed to win any more hearts and minds than the handful we'd started with, we signed a peace treaty we had no intention of living up to, went home, and spent the next twenty years doing our best to make sure the people who beat us would be unable to clean up the damage we'd left behind.

That's a long way from high school civics, to say the least.

I suppose each of us has his or her own version of who led us into that morass. My favorite candidate is John Wayne. He was just a movie actor, but I cannot imagine this war without him. John Wayne was the man those of us who were eventually called to take our turn out in the tall grass were supposed to be. We'd all been raised in his shadow.

It seems a little hard to believe now, when the Duke is little more than an occasional apparition on late-night cable, but at the time he was also a kind of short-hand yardstick for attitudes about the war.

When registration for military conscription was re-introduced for the first time since the end of the hostilities in Southeast Asia, I had been a working journalist for some seven years, and *The New York*

Times Magazine dispatched me to interview the first young man to be tried for draft resistance in the new post-Vietnam era. I asked him if it had been difficult to overcome his "John Wayne thing" in order to do what he did.

"What's a 'John Wayne thing'?" he responded.

Maybe it was just us. And maybe times had changed a whole lot in between. The war more or less ensured that much.

Today, when the dilemmas are often about multiplicity and the surplus of identities and options, it is hard to remember just how uniform everything was back when the Air Cavalry was first getting bloodied in the Ia Drang Valley and small demonstrations against the war were springing up on college campuses around the United States. But I remember. For all intents and purposes, it was still the fifties, and the options available to anyone in the culture at large fluctuated between few and none. For young men and boys, those options were conveniently reduced to a choice among John Wayne, John Wayne, and John Wayne. We were to say few words and say them with a growl, keep a hard jaw and a tight ass, not snivel, stifle feelings, take orders, never cry, dish out punishment to the bad guys, fire from the hip, know we were right just because we were Americans, always win, but die like heroes if our luck ran out. We were to be patriots, revere the flag, honor God and Country, and follow the chain of command. Anything other than that was a void. Those of us who eventually figured out that we wanted something besides what the chain of command was offering had to make our own options from scratch. That was not easy.

The truth was, whatever grander political opinions we might spout, we all had our own very personal John Wayne things to surmount before we could do much else. Getting the war out of the boy was every bit as much an issue as getting the boy out of the war. It meant a lot to refuse the chain of command in those days, and for most of us an internal transformation was necessary even to approach the act. We had to overcome an almost universally accepted dogma that it was disloyalty verging on treason for citizens to criticize the government when our soldiers were in combat. And, thanks in large part to the cinematic contributions of the Duke, being a man and being a good soldier were virtually synonymous in the generic Americanism practiced around Fresno and its like. So, before becoming antisoldiers, we all had first to come to terms with not being the soldiers we'd expected ourselves to be.

I had played high school football, wanted to be a career army officer when I was in elementary school, an FBI agent when I was in junior high. I was by no means unusual. Most of the draft resisters I knew had similar histories. We did, after all, believe in civics, and

John Wayneism was something of an unstated theme in that curriculum. The contract between the government and the governed was still largely intact, and disobedience was not in the lexicon. Until I left Fresno to go to college, I had never even heard the words "draft resistance." We were well prepared for soldierhood. We had been promised World War II to fight, and we were eager, but this war, it turned out, was different. Even a John Wayne movie about it didn't work.

That was *The Green Berets*, arguably among the worst the Duke ever made. In it he was a leader in the elite army counterinsurgency force that organized the Vietnamese—all of whom seemed to worship him in a monosyllabic way—into a "strategic hamlet," one of the new barbed-wired villages and patterns of forced relocation that were a mid-sixties staple in our war policy. In the movie, of course, no one was forced, and long lines of Vietnamese sought the sanctuary offered by the wise and friendly John Wayne and his buddies. The action was provided by night attacks from crazed villains in black pajamas who threw themselves on the barbed wire and got blown into various fractions of their hideous selves. As usual, John Wayne's character got nicked but toughed it out.

I actually laid eyes on the Duke himself not too long after *The Green Berets* came out. It was at one of those only-in-the-sixties events. A draft resister I knew, one of seven sons of an unemployed carpenter, was marrying the heiress to a dog food fortune, and I flew down to Orange County, to the airport that would eventually be named John Wayne International, and stood up with the groom. Both he and his bride had hair over their shoulders. The Duke, a friend of the bride's somewhat mortified parents, attended the reception. His hair was cut with sidewalls. My friend Jeffrey, another draft resister, was the first to spot him, his paunch parked against the mahogany bar while he finished off his second double Scotch. By the time Jeffrey got up the nerve to approach, the Duke was through his third. The veins on his nose had begun to swell, and he started to snarl when he saw Jeffrey coming. Then he muttered something about "fucking hippies." Jeffrey came back and said John Wayne was sloshed.

The Duke remained an icon until his end not so long ago.

Some of us will never forget you, John Wayne. Out in the tall grass, where so many poor boys breathed their last, more than a few of them died with your autograph on their souls.

4

I WAS NINETEEN when I demonstrated against the
war for the first time. It was the fall of 1965, when
the first rotation of American troops was still settling in around Saigon and Da Nang. I had been
in Mississippi the previous fall for a quick tour with
the civil rights movement, volunteering in the effort to
win black people the right to vote and put a final end
to Jim Crow, but the politics I had brought to it were
minimal and had grown only a little over the intervening year. I knew about the Geneva Accords by then,
about the obstruction of free elections, about Ho Chi
Minh, Bao Dai, and Ngo Dinh Diem. I knew about
napalm and strategic hamlets and the Demilitarized
Zone. I was, by then, eager to cross the line into open
opposition.

I remember the occasion was a march against the war, staged in Berkeley, under the theme "Get out of Vietnam." The original plan had been to march from the University of California to the Army Supply Depot on the Oakland waterfront, but the city of Oakland had denied a parade permit, so we marched to the border, where a line of Oakland police were waiting in riot gear, and held a rally on the Berkeley side, where we were watched by the combined Oakland and Berkeley police, plus a delegation of Alameda County Sheriff's deputies. Perhaps five thousand people attended, not counting cops, and some two hundred of those had driven up from Stanford, about equal parts student and faculty. A march the previous week along the same route had been attacked by several members of the Hell's Angels motorcycle gang. The bikers were out along the sidewalk again as we marched down the middle of the street, but nobody attacked. At the rally I remember a long-winded speech about how the United States had violated the Geneva Accords assuring the decolonization, independence, and unification of Vietnam. I caught a ride home afterward with a friend driving a VW van.

A decade of demonstrations followed: in front of federal buildings and outside napalm plants, induction centers, military bases, defense laboratories, troop depots, boot camps, airport gates, university auditoriums, think-tank campuses, assorted courthouses both state and federal, and both the Pentagon and the White House. I am still proud of most of them.

They were all the same in a way: we were just looking for a chance to open the discussion and conduct the argument. We were convinced that once anybody started taking a hard look at what was going on out in the tall grass, he or she would come to abhor it as much as we did. That certitude was a blessing, to be sure, but, like everything connected with this war, it became its own kind of burden as well. Few who came of age in those days got off easy. I remember.

The first step across the line felt like an emergence, from dark into light, from forest into clearing, instantly easing the groping pressure of trying first to suppress our disbelief and then, finally unable to suppress any longer, to endure the rub of mustering gumption sufficient to risk ourselves. Everyone in the Movement had a succession of those moments of initial elevation as each new risk was assumed. The one I remember best came in August 1966, some three months after I'd been elected student body president. I was living in a ramshackle house in East Palo Alto, about half a mile from the mud flats along San Francisco Bay. I shared the house with six others, but none of them was home. After thinking awhile, I sat at my typewriter and wrote a letter to my draft board back in Fresno. I enclosed my draft cards and told to whom it may concern at Local Board No. 71 that I would never carry them again, nor obey any of their orders as long as the war lasted. I sealed the envelope, walked down the block to the mailbox, and put the envelope in. I remember that summer afternoon, the dirt of the road shoulder, the enormous black walnut trees nearby, and I remember feeling like I could have flapped my arms and flown back to my house if I had wanted. I felt like I was my own man for the first time in my life.

I had, of course, jumped more than a few hurdles by then. I had not been raised to call attention to my complaints, so parading on a street to announce them to anyone who would listen was an extreme form of learned behavior. But I learned. I also learned to ignore the taboo against challenging the government in time of war. We all knew somehow that this was far too serious to stand back like that. In the early days, when there were only a very few of us in just a few places, most of us were liberated territory to one another. And there was not much else available. Estrangement from the norm was an almost universal condition among us, part of the disintegration the war spread all along the home front. The norm was dropping jellied gasoline on the tree line and firing canister rounds into thatched huts; life as we had been raised to live it had turned out to be a function of the chain of command. So we had to invent new selves as well: not an easy task for anyone at any time but especially difficult when swimming upstream against both our government and our culture.

None of us should have had to make such choices when we did. We were too young, and the choices were too hard. But we made them anyway. It was part of our victimization that we should come of age at the crux of our nation's moral fulcrum, where it would be left to us to stand up to the war on which our elders had decided to spend us. Most were not especially prepared for this role, but we had to play it, writing the script as we went along. We had to deal with the war, somehow figuring out if we were going to have a part in it or a part in stopping it and just what that part should be. The stakes were genuine, and the consequence seemed enormous. It was not something easily escaped. Some choices were enforced, whether you made them or not. If we did not act to make ourselves our own, we were the government's by default. And the wages of being your own were severe.

A year and a half after I sent my draft cards back, the FBI came by to talk. Since the door was open, they walked in without knocking. By then we had a printing press in the garage and had been organizing civil disobedience against the Selective Service System for more than six months, living from cereal boxes, most of the time on the road in my Rambler. The FBI said they were looking for David Harris. I said I was he, though they seemed to know that already. They said they wanted to talk. I said fine. They said out in their car, and I said fine again. They had me sit in the shotgun seat, with an agent behind the wheel and another behind me. They said I should know that whatever I said could be used against me. I said I had figured as much. They said they'd heard that I had been advocating that people violate the Selective Service Act. I said I certainly had and went through the previous month, day by day, providing places and times. I started to do the same for the month before, but the FBI said that was enough. They said they would be in touch.

I, of course, can never forget that the war was the law, and being against the war was treated as being against both. Nor should the rest of us forget it. That's just the way things were: to be young, scruffy, against the war, and outspoken was automatically to be treated as a suspect. From there it was a short step to outlaw, a step a lot of us made in a lot of different ways. And all those steps ended up a metaphor for the drift of the whole: we were forced to give up the comfort of the entrenched and the safety of silence and wander the badlands, looking for a place from which to hold off the forces of the tunnel without light at its end: outlaws of the heart at least.

We also have our own admissions with which to reckon: we sometimes drifted into the self-righteous, were plagued by a compulsion to push the envelope, to reinvent ourselves over and over again. We were faddists and could easily take ourselves too seriously and forget that our own position on the war had come at the end of a long and tormented personal migration. Too often our talk was cheap and our listening hard to come by. We latched onto simple truths no one else wanted to recognize and rode them until their wheels fell off. We were too quick to license all disbelief and too slow to reach outside our own presumptions. We were often too loud.

All that said, I still remember: we were also right.

After the war had been over for a short while, I was called before a Senate subcommittee. Jimmy Carter had just assumed the presidency, and the senators had convened a hearing to discuss those who had violated the wartime draft laws. I was asked to testify on the possibility of being given a pardon.

When I actually testified, no senators were present, all either replaced with uninterested aides or represented by empty chairs, so I made it short and to the point. I said a pardon was out of the question. I wasn't the one who had done anything wrong. But, if they were finally feeling penitent for all that had happened to me and to the country, I for one would accept a simple apology and their public promise never to do anything like that again.

Neither was offered, not then and not later, to absolutely no one's surprise.

I also remember that there was no predicting just whose mind would change about our war and when and where that change would happen. Some of the least likely came the furthest and transformed the most.

Ray certainly fit that category. Ray was my buddy during the summer of 1964, when I was about to start my sophomore year at Stanford and working as a short-order cook in a coffee shop in Sequoia National Park. Ray was the head busboy, a jock from Morro Bay, headed off to Hancock Junior College to play football. He was a fullback with thick shoulders, a thick neck, and a thick attitude. Kicking ass along the yard stripes was everything to him. I'd played ball with guys like Ray, so he and I laughed a lot, but we never discussed politics. Politics was dipshit stuff to Ray, though he was bright enough to know better. We were in Sequoia when the Tonkin Gulf Resolution was passed, but nobody talked much about the war in those days. Certainly Ray and I didn't. When the summer ended, I took his address but figured Ray would go on to his fullback dreams and I'd never come across him again. I was wrong on both counts.

Ray's football career never panned out the way he'd hoped, and by the time I headed off for prison he was headed for his second tour in the South China Sea as an enlisted man on the crew of the aircraft carrier USS *Kitty Hawk*. Out there the last time, he had helped dispatch the *Kitty Hawk*'s share of the air armada then intent on leveling as much of Southeast Asia as they could. When off watch, Ray spent a lot of time reading

and discovered Henry David Thoreau and Mahatma
Gandhi and the concept of nonviolent civil disobedience. By the time he and the ship were back in San
Diego, Ray's mind had changed, and, while the *Kitty
Hawk* was preparing to return and take up the cudgel
again, he decided to make that change of mind official. This war was wrong and he wanted no more part
of it. At the morning inspection he told his immediate
superior that he was tired of killing people and wanted
out of the navy. The officer laughed. The next day Ray
announced that he was refusing to report for duty and
beginning a hunger strike. He intended to maintain
his fast until his discharge or his death, whichever
came first. The ship's guard was summoned, and Ray
was immediately dispatched to the brig.

After twenty days of starving himself in the lockup,
Ray was taken out of his cell in chains and dog-walked
down one of the *Kitty Hawk's* gangplanks between two
lines of Marines: Ray clanking all the way, and each
and every Marine spitting on him and shouting after
him with epithets about what a chickenshit squab
motherfucker he was. Then Ray was turned and dog-
walked back through again with the grunts hanging a
second barrage of yellow lungers along the sides of his
head and down his neck. After thirty-two more days of
starving himself in the brig, Ray was moved to the
naval hospital, where he refused all attempts to sustain
him. His weight had fallen from 195 on the day he

announced he was through to 125 on the day he reached the hospital. The doctors said he was two days from dying. Then the navy said he would get a discharge. He said he wanted signed papers and waited another day, starving himself on the edge of death, for them to be processed.

Ray spent his first civilian months clawing his way back to health. He lost parts of his tongue, but otherwise he healed intact and the loss effected no lasting damage. He was chortling the same way he used to as a busboy when I ran into him again.

Ray told me he'd gotten tired of waiting on Nixon, so he had decided to make peace on his own. It just took a while to convince them he was serious.

The last demonstration against the war in which I ever participated took place in front of the American embassy in Saigon in early 1975, some three months before the former capital of the former Republic of Vietnam was renamed Ho Chi Minh City by the advancing ranks of infantry shod in sandals cut from old truck tires. The idea for the demonstration belonged to Tom, with whom I had organized during the last year before the Paris Agreements. Since then I had begun to write for a living, and when Tom called I was a contributing editor at *Rolling Stone*, about to turn twenty-nine years old. He said Congress was considering a fresh appropriation for the dying Thieu regime and the vote was coming up. He wanted someone with enough celebrity to draw the attention of the news wires for a picket of the American embassy in Saigon, protesting the appropriation request. Such demonstrations were illegal in the Republic of Vietnam, so I and the seven other Americans who would participate could count on being arrested. It was considered too dangerous for any Vietnamese to join in, but for us the most likely outcome was deportation. Tom thought the action might draw media, and the ensuing blurb on the evening news might help sway what promised to be a close vote.

I told Tom he must be down to the bottom of his celebrity barrel if he was hoping I would pull ink, but I went. Tom had money for my expenses, and I wanted to see the Republic of Vietnam before it was extinct. I landed at Tan Son Nhut Airport four days beforehand, passed through immigration with no hitches, and spent the four days moving around the city with the assistance of one of Tom's Saigon contacts, traveling usually by bus or pedicab to working-class neighborhoods, often down narrow rabbit-warren lanes, and never taking any of the Chevrolet taxis, which were thought to be manned largely by agents of Thieu, the American embassy, or both. Most of the city's major intersections were guarded by military police behind sandbags who stopped Vietnamese and checked their identity cards, looking for draft dodgers and deserters.

At that point there was an active front barely twenty miles outside town, where the North Vietnamese offensive was momentarily stalled. The protocol for our demonstration was that none of the participants was to make contact with the others until we were actually in front of the embassy. The American TV crews would be tipped an hour ahead of time so they could be there to film what we expected would be our immediate arrest.

The demonstration came off flawlessly, but our arrest was not so immediate. We stood in front of the embassy fence holding signs about the Thieu government and the American appropriation and distributing leaflets that had been translated into Vietnamese. The first police to arrive were members of the Saigon security forces, who drove white jeeps, wore white enameled helmets, and were nicknamed the White Mice. Under ordinary circumstances they would have swept us up pell-mell, but they saw a rank of American television crews across the street waiting for the action to commence and decided to talk with people inside the embassy first. In the meantime the street was awash with morning rush-hour traffic, and most who passed by did a double take at the confrontation. Hands reached out everywhere for leaflets, and before the standoff was an hour old all our leaflets were gone. So we just stood there for the rest of the morning and much of the afternoon, the eight of us on one side of the street with our signs and the White Mice with their nightsticks and the press corps with their cameras on the other.

In perhaps the greatest mystery of the event, a Vietnamese none of us knew, looking like an innocent pedestrian, walked by late in our sojourn, dropped off a load of leaflets, then disappeared into traffic without a word before the White Mice had any idea what was going on. The new batch of leaflets had the same text as those we'd distributed that morning, with just a sentence or two rewritten here and there. None of us ever found out who'd done this reprint, but we began to pass them out anyway.

The new leaflets helped force the issue. The White Mice were not going to allow a repeat of the morning, and when we began leafleting again they blocked the road and rerouted traffic so now only a four-lane expanse of bare asphalt separated us and there was no one else to leaflet. We and the White Mice stared at each other until the issue came to a head at 4:00 P.M., Saigon time, when the television network transmission deadline passed. Any film that was headed for that day's evening news had to be sent by 4:00, and at 4:01 our little eight-person event went from new news to old news. At 4:02 we were in custody. The White Mice drove us straight to the airport, hurried us through immigration, and put us on the next flight to Bangkok.

A day's travel later I was back in San Francisco, hugging Lacey in the airport. We had been with each other for only some five months then. That night as I lay in bed, awash with jet lag, she asked me if I had any more demonstrations in mind.

"No," I said, "I think I'm finally done."

5

WHEN IT WAS ALL OVER, our journey down the tunnel with no light at its end left most of us to start over in a different place—as though this were a biblical epic instead of a war movie, and God, infuriated by our transgressions, had cast us out to wander in the wilderness. I don't endorse such theories about heavenly judgment, but I am sure that if God had wanted to act that way toward the Americans, He had probable cause. Our arrogance was monumental.

We knew nothing about our destination, but we went anyway. We never did try to learn much once we were there. We had no idea that most Vietnamese national myths were accounts of long-term wars of national liberation waged against foreign invaders. We figured nobody with slant eyes could possibly stand up to the weight of American firepower, even though our last war had been against the slant eyed and they had fought us to a standstill. Our best generals had warned us against any infantry fight on the Asian mainland, but we began one anyway. We could have negotiated a settlement as early as 1964, but we wanted all or nothing. The Republic of Vietnam, our surrogate, had little support from its own people, but we figured several Ph.D.s from Harvard and Michigan State could sort it out. We thought we could fix anything that was broke and weather any storm that could possibly blow up over a backwater place like this. We thought they would love us because we drank Coca-Cola and let them drink it too. We thought we were too attractive to resist, too fierce to stop, and too smart to get lost.

There was more. We thought we could get by kidding ourselves about just how good we were. We were sure the enemy was being decimated because we had the best weapons money could buy. We had only the slightest idea what the enemy was up to, but we were sure that once we killed a few of them, the rest would just roll over. It never occurred to us that these people might hate us and find us ugly and foreign in every sense of the word. We were sure that we were the best thing God had to offer, and that we had the right to do whatever we did. So we did things for which we

would have killed anyone who came into our neighborhoods and did the same. We treated most of those
we encountered as less than ourselves. We made lots of
plans, but in all of them we placed little value on the
way of life that was being destroyed by our presence.
We thought they were lucky to have us and were upset
when they didn't say so. We thought that if they sold us
blow jobs, they must be on our side. We thought no
ten-year-old boy would ever throw a grenade into a
truck full of Americans; we thought no one would live
in tunnels underground for months just to get a
chance to put an AK-47 round through an American's
heart. We thought no army could last for long without
a PX. We thought we were "going for the gusto" and
"being the best we could be." And that, of course,
would be enough.

We thought we could generate sufficient suffering
to make them say "uncle." We thought we could bomb
them into the Stone Age. We thought we could pacify
them. We thought we could search them out and
destroy them. And when it turned out that we couldn't
do any of those things, we couldn't even admit it. Nor
could we admit that we often didn't know up from
down and were making a mess out of things. We
thought our interests had automatic precedence over
anyone else's. We thought we were civilized and they
weren't. We thought our purposes were sufficient
cause to poison their countryside. We couldn't fathom

that getting rid of us would be sufficient incentive to mobilize millions of people to risk everything. We thought we could win concessions at the bargaining table that we had never won on the field of battle. We thought we couldn't trust them but they could trust us. We thought that whatever we said was true just because we said it. We thought our government knew best. We thought our government would never tell us lies. We thought that if we escalated just a few more notches we'd have them right where we wanted them. We thought no one could match us toe to toe for a year, much less for ten. We thought what they did to our prisoners was shameful but thought nothing about what we did to theirs. We thought our surrogate government, still with little or no popular support, could resist the force that had kicked our ass for years. We thought we could save face by leaving the war with the South Vietnamese army still in the field. We also promised to repair war damage and normalize our relations after the war was over when we never had any intention of doing so.

And the last chapter was just as arrogant as the first. For twenty years after we fled from our embassy roof, we refused to officially recognize the government that had defeated us. We did so because we claimed they had failed to account sufficiently for our soldiers who were still listed as missing in action. In our own hysteria, we even suspected they might be holding live

Americans, though there was no credible evidence and they had no reason whatsoever to do so. We proclaimed that the Vietnamese attitude toward our list of perhaps three thousand still missing soldiers made them unfit for membership in the community of nations and said so even though we had, with their occasional assistance, already accounted for a far higher percentage of our missing in action than in any previous modern American war. We said so even though theirs was a culture of ancestor reverence in which the actual physical location of the dead's bodily remains is far more central to traditional spirituality than it is to ours and hundreds of thousands of their own soldiers and civilians were still unaccounted for. We said so even though, impoverished and ravaged, they had few if any means to search out those remains.

It was assumed that our few poor, lost boys, caught in paperwork limbo between here and gone, were worth far more than their multitudes.

Over and over in our war, we collided head-on with the Other.

We were the world's richest and the world's strongest, its most industrial, its most modern, its most technologized, and its most comfortable power. We had never been beaten. We were the creatures of advantage and prosperity. There had always been a relative few of us occupying a relatively large space. We were urban and suburban, motorized and televised, overfed and over-stimulated. We expected immediate gratification in all things. We were a nation of immigrants and migrators. We ate our food fast, kept our roots shallow, and frequently left our families behind. We followed fads and made our own rules, often as we went along. We believed our machines could solve our problems. We hadn't fought a war inside our own borders in a century, and it had been almost two centuries since we'd been a colony. Now we were a big-ticket item, the first of the First World.

And they, of course, were small change and as Third World as Third World could be. There had always been a lot of them in a relatively small place. They were traditional and hidebound, and most of them lived and expected to die in the same village on the same land where their parents had lived and died and their parents' parents as well. They were rural, remote, and redundant. They were also poor. They had been resisting colonization by one set of foreigners or another for more than a millennium and had never fought a war anywhere but close to their homes. They walked and waded and worked and wasted nothing. They had little choice but to put gratification off until they could afford it. They had no industry to speak of, one highway, one railroad, and millions of bicycles. They dreamed of paddies and plantations. They were creatures of disadvantage and hardship. Most could neither read nor write, and most ate sparsely, respected their elders, and valued endurance over speed.

And, of course, they were yellow skinned and slant eyed. We expected that a land full of dinks — most of whom still drew their water out of wells in buckets — would scatter at our approach like a bunch of terrified Kiowa encountering their first iron horse. We thought the sophistication and grit required for a serious military effort would be beyond people whose men held hands, whose women dug canals, and whose children had never seen a TV. We expected a slant-eyed cross between Charlie Chan, Madame Butterfly, and Mr. Moto who would recognize their inferiority and surrender when it actually dawned on them just who they would have to fight. We assumed that we were much more suited for putting their affairs in order than they were. They, on the other hand, were much more suited to tasks like planting rice. And we expected they would accept both assumptions.

In our caricature, they placed little value on human life; accordingly, we placed little value on theirs. We imagined they would fight us with human wave attacks, seeking to overwhelm us with numbers, and never imagined that they would outsmart us as well. We pictured the Asian mind as conniving, unscrupulous, and brutal but never as incisive or brilliant. We could not tell one of them from another, so we assumed tens of millions of people were all the same and treated them that way. We considered them primitive and superstitious. We took their Oriental inscrutability for granted, giving us an excuse never to know who they really were and making both bombing them and buying sex from their daughters much easier than it would have been otherwise. They were different from Americans, and we assumed that meant they were worse.

The conundrum for us, of course, was that we were also different from one another and assumed much the same things about ourselves. Our army ranged all the way from shoe polish to Wonder bread, a diversity that framed a subplot of the very same dilemma that helped bring us to Vietnam. That part of it at least was an old American story. At the time of the Tonkin Gulf Resolution, blacks in Alabama and Mississippi were still being lynched for trying to register to vote, and by the Tet Offensive the black corners of America's cities were often on fire and occasionally occupied by the National Guard. By the time of the 1972 Christmas bombings, one fragment of our army in Vietnam was giving each other the Black Power salute while another was whistling Dixie and flying the Stars and Bars.

And perhaps the only common ground between them was their shared belief that whatever the racial pecking order might be among our native niggers, honkies, slopes, and greasers, they all had the right to do just about whatever they felt like to the gooks who actually lived there. So we did to them as we were in the habit of doing to one another, only much, much worse.

That daisy chain may have been as crazy as any of the things we stumbled into out in the tall grass; certainly it was as ugly.

Nowhere was the collision more archetypal than over the Ho Chi Minh Trail.

This "trail" was in fact a network of interlacing trails, sometimes wide enough to run heavy trucks, sometimes with leeway for nothing larger than a bicycle. The network ran north to south, down through the rugged Annamite mountain chain that binds North Vietnam, Laos, Cambodia, and South Vietnam, mountains that reach all the way to the South China Sea at several places. Otherwise the Vietnamese coastal plain occupies one flank of the Annamites, and the middle Mekong Valley of southern Laos and eastern Cambodia occupies the other. The Annamites are at places an almost impenetrable collection of slopes and gorges, rising as high as five thousand feet and covered by triple-canopy forest, but the trails running through them became the principal avenue for the other side's logistics during the war's escalation toward the 1968 Tet Offensive. War goods from the Soviet Union, China, and the Eastern Bloc, and rice and staples from North Vietnam itself flowed south to fuel the main force units of the NLF and the increasing number of North Vietnamese army troops operating out of redoubts in the central highlands, just north of the malaria-ridden Plateaux Montagnards.

The Ho Chi Minh Trail posed a significant problem for American planners throughout the war, but doing something about it was no simple matter. The obvious solution of occupying the territory through which the trail ran was out of the question. Inserting and maintaining a force of the size that would be required was beyond us. We faced a fierce fight under the worst possible conditions simply to get close to the trail and faced a potential military disaster if it didn't work out quite like we planned. It was difficult for us even to tell what was moving along the trail and when. The triple canopy hid everything.

Our solution was to unleash our machines. The assault began with the distribution of Air-Delivered Seismic Intrusion Detectors, known as ADSIDs and dropped from radar-guided F-4 Phantom jets. The ADSID was a listening device, a yard long and six inches thick, designed to fall freely and bury its point into the earth with a broadcast antenna that stuck up and looked like underbrush. The battery in each lasted for more than a month, and its electronics, in the ground, detected movement and radioed that detection to a small propeller-driven air force plane that relayed it to a much larger propeller-driven plane stuffed with electronics, which, in turn, relayed it to an infiltration surveillance center. That center also received information from reconnaissance flights by our F-4 Phantom jets and by several remotely piloted drones. This info was all processed by an enormous IBM mainframe computer, which then recommended air strikes. And off went the Phantoms, now loaded with ordnance, and even the B-52s sometimes, making the ground tip and the forest shiver.

They countered our machines with people and more people and more people. The heart of their system was a corps of tens of thousands of porters, each of whom could carry 55 pounds on his or her back for an average of fifteen miles a day where the country was flat and nine miles a day in the mountains. These porters also pushed modified bicycles over sections of the trail, and each of those bikes could carry 150 pounds. The sections of the trail big enough for trucks were piled with battered Soviet ZILs. Workshops and mechanics were stationed along the road to keep them running, as were road repair crews. When the trail was damaged by the American bombardment, a crater was immediately swarmed upon by men and women furiously moving dirt in baskets, digging with hoes and shovels, and filling it so the flow south could resume.

The outcome was never really in doubt. After attacking the Ho Chi Minh Trail daily for ten years, we never closed it, we never forced it to move, we hardly even delayed traffic along it for more than twenty-four hours. Embarrassing as our failure was, we should nonetheless remember: we would have taken that failure as almost heartwarming if the identical archetype had belonged to anybody but us.

One of the mysteries I have grappled with in the decades since the war is just what was the belief that sustained our body politic through it all. The tunnel with no light at its end was an extraordinarily long haul, especially since, for most of its duration, we suspected it was a waste. Faith of some sort was obviously required. I do not, of course, mean *professed* faith: that was mostly ideology and public relations: anticommunism, Mom, apple pie, and the chain of command. I mean what we really believed: the conviction held along our backbones and turned to when danger approached: our resort under pressure, what made us feel safe, our instinctive response, what we reached for first, where we daily looked when we needed to muster hope. Most of the answers I landed on at the onset were illusions: we did not have faith in anticommunism, no matter how much we swore by it. The same was true of the apple pie, Mother, and the chain of command. Boys hunkering under incoming found little refuge in repeating mantras provided by the John Birch Society or invoking the name of their commander in chief. Whatever solace those sources might provide, no one for a minute believed that any of them could do much when we needed help most.

Finally, I turned for my answer to our behavior, looking for acts of faith rather than declarations. I tried to examine what we did in reality and locate the faith I hoped to identify inside those acts looking out. Perhaps it wasn't so complex after all; perhaps we believed in just what we acted like we believed in.

By that standard we believed in firepower, pure and simple.

When push came to shove, we worshiped at the temple of the Quad 50: four M-2HB Browning .50 caliber machine guns fired simultaneously, a total of some eighteen hundred rounds per minute, each capable of penetrating an inch of armor plate at a thousand yards; we prayed to the BLU-1/B napalm canister: ninety gallons of jellied gasoline blended with plastic, dropped by dive-bombers, each canister capable of frying a chunk of the tree line and everyone in it; we sought refuge in the M-108 self-propelled 105-mm howitzer: dug in behind sandbags, throwing a 50-pound XM-546 antipersonnel shell up to eight miles. We believed in being able to shoot anything that moved, anywhere, anytime we wanted to shoot it. We also believed in shooting first and asking questions later. We called out in our need to the F-4 Phantom, capable of flying fourteen hundred miles an hour, carrying eighteen M-117

750-pound bombs or eleven Mk-83 1,000-pound bombs or a whole mess of the good old BLU-1/Bs, and we genuflected to the Bell AH-1 Cobra, a helicopter with a front-mounted six-barreled M-134 7.62-mm minigun, capable of firing four thousand rounds a minute, and two side-mounted M-158 2.75-inch rocket pods, each firing seven rockets within six seconds with a range of 3,750 yards.

We believed that there was no such thing as a surplus of force and used it with such abandon that the other side considered the safest place on the battlefield to be as close to the Americans as possible, where our options were narrowed to standard infantry weapons and our machines had to respect the proximity of our own troops. Otherwise, we made a point of raining death at the least provocation. When in doubt blast it, plaster it, waste it, blow it away; cut it down, fuck it up, ream it, cream it, beam it up; deal it the ace of spades; drop it, bop it, pop it, then lay on the big one and another for its mama; pull the switch, finger the trigger, line up the sight, measure the range, drive a cold one home; feed it lead like you are out of your head until you are very sure it is dead.

The saints of our faith were legion: the M-60 7.62-mm general-purpose machine gun, five hundred rounds per minute; the M-34 incendiary fragmentation grenade, lethal fragments within thirty meters, white phosphorus within forty-one; the M-7A2 antipersonnel

mine, explosion equivalent to a direct hit of a round
fired by an M-108 105-mm howitzer. And new saints
arrived weekly: we designed a bomb called the Daisy
Cutter whose explosion dug a crater the size of half a
city block; we built a propeller-driven plane called Puff
the Magic Dragon that mounted a gun rig in its open
side door and delivered up to twenty thousand rounds
a minute; we invented a smart bomb that followed a
laser beam to its target; we even spread antipersonnel
mines that lay openly on the ground and were dis-
guised to look like dog turds, each one capable of blowing someone's feet off. In the fervor of our worship, we
quite literally splintered the landscape. We left forests
reduced to stumps and, using chemicals sprayed in
blankets from low-flying aircraft, denuded more than a
million acres of vegetation in a program euphemisti-
cally named Operation Ranch Hand. As a standard
operating procedure, our first call was to fire support,
and the subsequent incoming friendlies splattered paddies, reduced orchards to pulp, plantations to mulch,
and savanna to burnt stubble and dirt clods. We blasted
crater upon crater upon crater, taking communion in
the Church of the Free-Fire Zone, and Vietnamese are
still blowing their feet off, stepping on ordnance we
"delivered" thirty years earlier.

We quite rightfully expected all that firepower
would prove our salvation, but we were wrong about
that too. Our faith was to no avail. And that was just

one of our war's many far less than storybook endings: firepower turned out to have limits even faith couldn't cure, and we, having taken our best shot, had nothing much left to believe in once our war had ground to a halt.

One of the ways we insulated ourselves from the implications of what we were doing was with language. Slaughter from ten thousand feet became an "air interdiction of hostiles"; leveling village after helpless village became "destroying the social infrastructure"; and those villages' occupants didn't live in them but "infested the area." We constructed phrases that had no compelling pictures attached and used them to hide the human face of the war as best we could.

In addition, everybody had bits and pieces of personal language for the same purpose.

Leonard's favorite was "zero product."

Leonard lived with his mother in Kansas City when I met him. He had been living there since he came back from Vietnam twenty years earlier. Leonard was one of the early ones "in country," operating in Saigon with a plainclothes military intelligence group before the Tonkin Gulf Resolution. A vet I knew put us together, saying Leonard had some interesting stories to tell. One sunny morning I talked to him, sitting on an old stuffed chair and sofa in an enclosed porch. Leonard was so skinny his bones showed, his hands shook a little, his fingers were lined with tobacco stains, and his teeth were a shade of brown. He had three ballpoint pens in his shirt pocket.

Once during our conversation he left and came back with a photograph in an old metal frame. It showed a much younger Leonard in a short-sleeved polyester shirt standing next to a Vietnamese woman he referred to as Tiny. She had died right before he came home, he said. At the time his unit had been "operating" against a network of NLF suspects, blowing them up as a warning. Leonard's job was to stroll by the bombing site as soon afterward as possible and make an initial assessment. His boss's code was a scale of "product." A "hundred product" meant they'd accomplished everything they set out to. "Zero product" meant they hadn't accomplished anything. On this particular day a bomb was supposed to be planted inside a coffee bar in Cholon, where a particular man came every day. The bomb, however, went off outside by mistake. When Leonard cruised up, almost at the same time as the police, the man who'd been assigned the job of planting the bomb was in smoldering pieces all over the roadside. Several passersby were in similar postures. One of them was Tiny. Her head had been blown clean off her shoulders and was lying in the coffee bar's front doorway. Her eyes already looked like fish eggs.

"It was zero product," Leonard said, fumbling for a cigarette and scratching a flame out of his Zippo.

"It was zero product," he repeated. "Zero."

Leonard seemed to expect the incantation to lighten his unease, but it didn't, so he took a deep drag, put his Zippo back in his pocket, and repeated himself again.

"It was zero product," he said. "The first zero product I'd ever been a part of."

Leonard's head was framed in tobacco smoke.

"Zero product," he repeated, looking nowhere in particular, "just plain zero."

Hurt is a difficult memory to pass on to those who did not experience it firsthand, and those of us who did experience it often hurt far too much to remember all of it, especially those men who had to live it up close at a time when most were still boys.

They hurt the hurt of the pointless sacrifice, of the wasted hero, the hurt of the discarded standard issue of a war machine that clearly had little idea which end was up or just what was worth saving and what was worth blowing to bits. They knew better than anyone that the machine's principal product was corpses made from boys just like themselves. And they ached from having their lives dangled over the abyss daily and having nothing to show for those who fell in; they throbbed with meaninglessness at their best, rampages of terror at their worst. They missed the world, regular TV, their girlfriends and boyfriends, their convertibles, their youth. They yearned for normalcy, quiet, and, above all else, safety. And if none of those was available, they would settle for being numb. Theirs was the pain of those slowly strangling on the substance of their daily lives, like patients suddenly turned allergic to themselves. Just how far that suffering had spread was not quite clear until 1970, when large amounts of medicine for the self-treatment of pain became directly available to our troops. The ensuing consumption was a remarkable bellwether.

The "medicine" in question was 80 to 98 percent pure, fine-grained, number-4 grade heroin. Coarse number-3 grade, still a complex refining process away from street use, had been an established product in the Golden Triangle—an area shared by Laos, Burma, China, and northern Vietnam—ever since the Americans started mucking around there. In the 1950s we had sponsored a Chinese warlord's army in northern Burma to harass the Communist Chinese, and that army had eventually turned to opium production. As part of our surrogate arrangement, we hauled the crop, already refined to number-3 grade heroin, out to Vientiane, Laos, on Air America, the CIA's airline. Air America also hauled the crop of our highland allies the Hmong tribesmen, again to Vientiane. From there it was smuggled into Saigon, then shipped to Hong Kong or Marseilles for final processing into number 4, and then distributed to the rest of the world.

Most of the heroin smuggling between Laos and Saigon was controlled by the highest level of the Republic of Vietnam's armed forces, though until 1970 Saigon was largely just a transit point between processors and there was little in the way of consumable heroin from that traffic left in country. The smuggling franchise was one of the plums of power in Saigon, and in the Republic of Vietnam's 1970 "election"—a staged show for the American home front in which no one was free to vote for anyone except the choice given by the government—the two candidates for president, the ARVN (Army of the Republic of Vietnam) general and incumbent Nguyen Van Thieu and the air force vice marshal Nguyen Cao Ky, were both involved in two of the nation's principal heroin-trafficking rings.

The big change that started supplying consumable heroin to our troops began during that 1970 campaign, when a Laotian general, the former commander in chief of our surrogate force in Laos and one of the chief heroin forwarders in Vientiane, finished construction of a refinery for processing fine-grained number 4 from the number 3 coming out of the mountains. The general's cover was his Laotian Pepsi-Cola franchise. More refineries soon followed.

The second key element in the coming outburst of American self-medication was the change in Cambodia. The regime of Prince Norodom Sihanouk had always suppressed heroin traffic, so the only route out of landlocked Laos was over the rugged highlands and into central Vietnam, where steep, tiny trails limited the volume that could be moved. There were only a few air flights to circumvent the bottleneck, so all the ongoing air smuggles had to be both complex and limited. The 1970 advent of Lon Nol, the new American puppet in Cambodia, transformed that. Suddenly Vientiane-refined number-4 heroin could be moved in an easy journey by land to Phnom Penh, to which the South Vietnamese army and air force now flew scheduled transports daily as part of joint ARVN and Cambodian operations. Those transports began returning to Vietnam with large caches of number 4, and the self-medication by desperate grunts suddenly increased exponentially.

By late 1970 small plastic vials of number 4 were available along every paved road between American bases, from every madam in every one of the brothels that ringed them, and from most of the mama-sans who came on base to clean hootches. The preferred form of consumption was usually smoking or snorting, since needles leave scars and, hence, evidence of use. Soon our army was blowing skag left and right. In one U.S. Army draftee division at the end of that year, a survey by the medical staff indicated 15 percent of the enlisted ranks had already tried heroin and some 7 percent were using it regularly. Six months later army doctors estimated that somewhere between 10 and

15 percent of the 250,000 troops still in Vietnam were consuming number 4. Other contemporary estimates were as high as 30 percent.

The poor boys in question paid four dollars or so American for a vial of the smuggled painkiller, and three or four vials a day was a standard habit. The slice of the traffic owned by General Thieu and Air Vice Marshal Ky and their cronies in the Republic of Vietnam's military command was worth some $90 million (1970 dollars) a year, much of which ended up in either Swiss banks or very large domestic stashes of gold bars, already packaged for quick travel.

And, in one of the uglier ironies in a war known for its ugly ironies, the same suffering soldiers who lost themselves in number 4 and who paid all the money that the general and air vice marshal made were also the ones required to fight to the death for the right of the general and the air vice marshal to make all that money off of them. Trapped in that kind of logic, it is no wonder those boys hurt as much as they did.

The ongoing irony of our self-enforced insulation from the pain and hurt of our war was that it was easily the most visible war the United States had ever fought: the Television War, a title once pronounced as though war and television were a unique combination. We take their symbiosis for granted now, as though every American rumpus room always had a window into military combat. Believe me, it didn't. At least not until this war heated up.

When trying to remember it, we mustn't forget the really simple stuff. This was, after all, a long time ago: America's video age, now well into its adulthood, was just in its adolescence then, and in Vietnam, out among the mangroves and the red dirt, the small screen had its first chance to cover the nation at war. There were three networks and not much else. They all broadcast their evening news at the same hour, and most of America watched. The war ran every night, night after night after night.

And the television reporters spoke a new language: of firefights, armored personnel carriers, M-16s, Vietcong, *di di mau*, buying the farm, door gunners, Hueys, teach-ins, medevacs, the Air Cav, I Corps, the DMZ, body counts, flak vests, Khe Sanh, Dienbienphu, number one and number ten, rice paddies, berm, strategic hamlets, RPGs, tree lines, gooks, concertina wire, claymores, peace marches, grenade launchers, the Geneva Accords, hootches, fatigues, free-fire zones, bunkers, Quad 50s, deuce and a halfs, short timers, cadre, grunts, sappers, walking point, getting iced, guerrillas, draft dodgers, sympathizers, suspects, POWs, deserters, tunnel rats, the Delta, Charlie, the Ho Chi Minh Trail, ARVNs, skag, peaceniks, flattops in the South China Sea, air bases in Thailand, doves in the Senate, negotiators in Paris, enlisted men fragging officers, Canadian exile, smart bombs, napalm, R and R, catching the big bird home.

With that language came a new set of images, often more startling than many in the audience had ever experienced before: Americans leaping out chopper doors, machine gunners firing at something invisible on the horizon, bloody grunts being dragged from the line of fire, starched generals at Saigon briefings speaking definitively of the pain being inflicted on the enemy, the flat patchwork of paddies spread in front of the hovering Huey, dead VC laid out on the road after a firefight, lucky marines grabbing a ride on an APC, shirtless dog soldiers with Marlboros in their helmet netting holding a Budweiser in one hand and a grenade launcher in the other, the president on prime time from the Oval Office with yet more war news, the smoke lifting off the airstrip as the North Vietnamese howitzer rounds whined in, the piles of dead boys waiting in the mud for a detail to bag them up, the long boxes being off-loaded at California air bases. And, of course, groups of scruffy-looking college students carrying signs outside the hotel where the vice president was delivering his speech or in front of the induction center.

We were by no means prepared for any of this. Nobody had anticipated it, not much we'd learned had led us to believe that what was happening was even possible. One minute it was *The Adventures of Ozzie &*

Harriet, the next it was true grit and the last throes of young grunts everywhere we looked. The war just seemed to drop in out of nowhere to hijack our sensibilities between commercials. That it made such a deep and lasting impression is no surprise. And, while only a small share of the responsibility belonged to television itself, the advent of the war on the dinner hour broadcast put life as we'd known it on its ear and left it there. All of our nightmares about it now have eighteen-inch Zeniths in them, flickering against the far wall.

We must not forget: it was a more simpleminded age, the information superhighway was still a deer trail, and network television was taken as reality, giving the folks back home a vivid, utterly riveting look at what some of their boys were going through, a kind of visceral access available to no previous generation of Americans.

To accompany those sights and sounds, the folks back home were also given a running explanation of what was going on from their government. And the latter created the war's second front. Unprecedented visibility ensured that in this war, the government fought one front in the paddies against its NLF and North Vietnamese adversaries and another over the U.S. airwaves, trying to put the appropriate spin on events and convince America that there really was some important reason for going through all this. There wasn't enough political support for the war to do otherwise, and television had too much impact. The obvious consequence was that Lyndon Johnson and then Richard Nixon spent a good deal of their energy playing to the cameras, just trying to make the war look like what America thought its wars should look like.

The result was a running feel-good scenario, mouthed from lots of official angles. The boys were fighting like true champions and they had to be supported. It was too bad there were nervous Nellies and cowards out there impeding the war effort, but thanks to loyal American boys, we were forcing the VC to pay an extraordinary price in the field. They were dying at a ratio that might well be as high as ten to one. At this rate there would soon be light at the end of the tunnel. The South Vietnamese government was making great progress, and the ARVN, its army, was taking an increasingly important role. They'd been out there in the field giving Charlie a bloody nose regularly. The enemy was being taught the hard way that aggression does not pay. We were steadily destroying their capacity to fight. Enemy control of the countryside was slipping. Victory was just around the corner. Perhaps by this Christmas . . .

As Christmas after Christmas passed, the message was delivered with a desperation that increased in lockstep with its preposterousness. We were being fought to a stalemate from the first day we touched down next to the South China Sea, but it was years before anyone with status was prepared to go on the tube and say so. Television has a propensity to mangle the messenger along with the message, so the only news anyone in Washington wanted to talk about was good news. Preoccupied with the war as a public-relations problem, the government essentially took the attitude that if something did not appear on the evening news, it did not happen. And so, tailored for television consumption, the American state lost its last handhold on reality and was soon just recycling its own projections.

Meanwhile, of course, the rest of the country watched from the safety of the Nielsen ratings, voyeurs at our own undoing.

Not only was it hard to know *what* was really going on but it was even hard to know *how* we would know what was really going on if we stumbled over it. All that craziness had compromised the nation's epistemology, rendering our accustomed patterns of knowing dysfunctional. In that sense, we were often literally senseless, stripped of the means to comprehend.

That said, every now and then something happened that suddenly made it all clear, much too clear. The Tet Offensive that began on January 31, 1968, and ended almost a month later was the mother of all such epiphanies. Named for the five-day Vietnamese New

Year's holiday during which it fell, this attack by the National Liberation Front was a singular event.

Throughout that fall of 1967, American commanders and, of course, the American commander in chief had evinced great confidence in how the war was going. We had then been in Vietnam in force for some two years. Search-and-destroy missions were hunting the enemy in the countryside, and the urban coastal corridor was under the firm control of the Republic of Vietnam. The villages were being pacified, and, according to escalating body counts we had been collecting, the Vietcong were suffering heavy attrition and would soon be in danger of extinction. Clearly only the North Vietnamese Army was keeping Charlie in the game at all, and that would not be enough. Daily air strikes were now being conducted by the hundreds, carpet bombing had been introduced, and the enemy's logistics along the Ho Chi Minh Trail were under tremendous pressure. As Christmas passed, a few Johnson administration insiders went so far as to make off-the-record assurances that by the next Christmas the war would be well in hand and American troop levels significantly reduced.

No such statements were being leaked on February 1, 1968. By then it was apparent that, far from disappearing, the VC were attacking in spades. Thirteen provincial capitals in the Mekong Delta were under assault, dozens of district seats had been seized by insurgents from there to the Central Highlands, and all the significant centers along the coast—Quang Tri, Hue, Da Nang, Hoi An, Quang Ngai, Qhinhon, and Nha Trang—were attacked as well. The American naval base at Cam Ranh Bay was shelled, and Saigon itself was the scene of short but intense small-unit and gunship firefights in which Vietcong commandos even penetrated the grounds of the American embassy. The longest fight raged in Hue, where NLF and NVA regulars held the old imperial Citadel—just down the Perfume River from Thien Mu Pagoda—for three and a half weeks, until they were overwhelmed by American firepower.

By then our home front was in a shambles, the war's credibility mortally wounded, and Lyndon Johnson's political future destroyed. The enemy that was supposed to be on its last legs had jumped from nowhere to everywhere and caught us totally by surprise. In the aftermath there were few doubts left that we were in for a long, hard fight. Within weeks Walter Cronkite, anchor of the *CBS Evening News* and the most trusted public figure in America, toured Vietnam and announced that the war was unwinnable. We fought for five years after that, but the issue for us for all that time was never *whether* to get out but only *how*.

In the decades since, a body of criticism has developed among the war's diehards that blames the press for our failure and cites the Tet Offensive as prime evidence. The Vietcong suffered tremendous losses, they point out, sacrificing a whole generation of their best troops to stand and make just the kind of bloody fight they had previously avoided at all costs. Their internal objective of triggering a national uprising had been a complete failure as well. We had lured them into exactly the battle we wanted, and then the press had turned tail and treated it all like a defeat.

Their complaint is by now an archetype: still arguing as though wars are won on scorecards and we'd been robbed by the judges. Our Vietnamese enemies had fought a colonial war before, they knew who they had to convince, and the Tet Offensive sent a message that reverberated from Des Moines to Dallas, Los Angeles to New York, Kansas City to Tallahassee, San Diego to Des Moines. It didn't matter who delivered the news. We had clearly bitten off more than we had been planning to chew. Since Johnson's government had already staked its policy on such an attack being impossible, it was defeated as soon as the Tet Offensive began. Then, with his Vietnam assessment exposed as little more than a remake of the Easter Bunny, Johnson's domestic flank rolled up and his political career came to a premature end. All the feel-good scenarios in Washington were now shot full of holes, and our capacity to sustain the necessary fight would never be the same. From Tet on, our own vulnerability was our leading concern and minimizing it the only sure political option. I suspect the attack would have been accounted our adversaries' victory had they paid twice or three times the price.

The Tet message took dozens of forms as it spread, but perhaps the most compelling was a wire-service photo from the fighting in Saigon. The photo featured two men: the first a balding South Vietnamese police general in tailored fatigues, the second a captured National Liberation Front commando in civilian pants, sandals, and a checked civilian shirt. The commando's arms were tied behind him, and he faced the camera. He was shorter than the general, whose back was to the camera with his right arm extended straight toward the right side of the commando's head. The general's profile was sighting down his arm. In his right hand was a hammerless chrome revolver with a snub nose, its short barrel aimed just above the commando's ear. The camera captured the instant the general's finger squeezed the trigger. His bound captive's head showed traces of a shrug and then a flinch at the bullet's first impact.

In this captured moment, consumed over and over again on our home front, the general seemed the slicker, the commando the more homespun, like half of Mr. and Mrs. Saigon, plucked off any of the city's street corners. I still remember the expression on his face: he looked as though we would have to blow the brains out of everyone like him if we were to have any hope of winning this.

The war was crazy, especially for those of us who lived through it.

We remember the U.S. Army major who, after a fierce fight over a place called Ben Tre, said that he had been forced to destroy the village in order to save it.

We remember that both Lyndon Johnson and Richard Nixon ran as peace candidates.

We remember that bombs were shipped in crates saying DO NOT DROP, that conscription was called service, that bringing the war to the countryside was called pacification, that we went ten thousand miles from home to a place that had never heard of the American Way in order to defend that Way, as if Cleveland was at stake. We remember that groups of armed men were dispatched to "win hearts and minds" and that groups of Vietnamese fighting on their own doorsteps were considered part of a foreign invasion of their country. We remember that Stalinist North Vietnam was called the Democratic Republic of Vietnam and that totalitarian South Vietnam, where there'd never been even the hint of a free election, was the "defender of democracy." We remember that our assassination program was run through a public agency for "international development" and that battlefield torture was a function of "military intelligence." We remember that poor boys killed by their own side were considered victims of "friendly fire."

Not much about any of it made sense, but it happened.

Over the years that nonsensical quality to our memories has helped insulate us. Those were crazy times, we say, often with a kind of uneasy chuckle, as though there is therefore no need to attempt to make further sense of it, as though the diagnosis alone was sufficient. In truth, that it was crazy is no excuse, no explanation, and hardly breaking news. Crazy or not, it was us. We need to claim that madness along with all the rest.

Our dementia took a myriad of forms, but behind them all was a kind of enabling delusion that made the rest of our delusions possible: We believed we could make anything we did into anything we wanted it to be just by explaining it that way; as though we could practice a kind of verbal alchemy, turning pigs' ears into platinum with the incantation of noble intentions; as though we were not bound by the chain of molecular events in which death and pain are the immutable lowest human denominators; as though we really could save places by destroying them; as though any means could yield any end, just so long as we said it did. This was, of course, madness of the first order, and, marching along under that moon, we stumbled through the charnel pit, waiting for the light to show up that would reveal it all to be a truly noble enterprise. It never did. The carnage was all there was, and it was madness to think we could believe it into something else.

And now, so much later, everything having been so crazy often makes remembering like looking through murky water. And that was just the way it seemed when it happened. It was indeed hard to make sense of it, and everyone's life back then was dotted with moments in which the world always seemed turned on its head. The one I remember best happened in the middle of August 1969.

I had been in the custody of the attorney general for almost a month then, locked up until the day before in a federal cellblock on the seventh floor of the San Francisco County Jail. For the preceding week the block had been on a hunger strike over the suspension of visiting privileges. I had been one of the strike's instigators. Then, in the middle of the afternoon, the cops handed me my street clothes and said the federal marshals were here for me. The marshals ran a chain through the belt loops of my Levi's, linked its two ends with my handcuff chain, and then cuffed my wrists to my waist. Once they got me into the backseat of their car, they shackled my ankles to each other as well, using leg cuffs over my cowboy boots. They then drove over the Bay Bridge to Oakland and took me to a maximum-security cellblock on the top floor of the Oakland courthouse. The only other resident on the block was a member of the Black Panther Party who was still recovering from wounds he'd received in a police shoot-out the year before. The next morning the marshals returned for me. This time, they said, we were headed for Arizona.

Again my wrists were shackled to my waist, and I was hustled into the elevator. In the Oakland court-house, the top-floor cellblock was serviced by the same elevator that serviced the rest of the building, and a woman who looked to be in her thirties got in at one of the civilian floors as we descended. She looked me up and down. I hadn't shaved in a week, and my work shirt hung on me like I had slept in it, which I had. I'd had no breakfast, and dinner the night before had been only my second meal in a week. I was flanked by two suits with faces like pit bulls'. I couldn't raise my hands above my bottom rib and then only both together and with a great clanking.

The woman got her courage up about the fourth floor and asked me what I'd done to get all chained up like that.

I shrugged. "I didn't kill anybody," I said.

6

—

LOOKING BACK ON IT now, at age fifty, I can see
that the force impelling me to take my stand
against the war drew strength from many
sources, but the stories of torture touched
me in a way nothing else quite did.

This was not the way Americans were supposed to
fight: manipulating the pain of the helpless, degrading
our adversaries, liberating nothing and no one, aban-
doning all notions of fairness and mercy. Nazis tortured, Tojos tortured, Stalinists tortured, but not
Americans. There was no footage in *Victory at Sea*
of marines forcing water down a Japanese prisoner's
throat, no money spent in Lend-Lease for rubber
hoses, finger needles, and thumbscrews. This behavior

was truly beyond all the combined boundaries set for us in high school civics, Sunday school, and the Boy Scout manual. But we did it nonetheless, from the first day we were there until the day we left: we broke arms, lifted fingernails, peeled skin with lit cigarettes, hung people by their thumbs, jumped on their stomachs until something burst, choked them within an inch of their lives, locked them in tiny cages that twisted their spines and withered their limbs. On occasion we took suspects in helicopters up to cruising altitude and threw the recalcitrant ones out the open chopper door when they refused to divulge what we wanted to know. We tortured the young and the old, we tortured both women and men. We trained our South Vietnamese protégés how to do it right and spent millions of dollars of the Agency for International Development's budget building some forty-four regional torture centers to make the process more efficient. Most of the suspects who lived to tell about it finished the war as cripples. And I suspect that many of those among us who participated in that torture dream about it to this day.

I had direct contact with that ugly national "secret" twice while the war was going on, once early in the fighting and once very late.

The first encounter was toward the end of 1966 or early in 1967, during the trial of an early draft resister in a federal courtroom in San Jose. The draft resister was defending himself by claiming the war was a violation of the Nuremberg precedent and wanted to call a recently discharged army sergeant as a witness. The sergeant had spent a tour out in the bush with a military intelligence unit that handled prisoners. As part of a hearing to determine its admissibility, the judge listened to some of the sergeant's testimony while the jury was out.

Had the sergeant seen prisoners tortured?

He had. Usually the actual hands-on stuff was done by the South Vietnamese while the Americans watched or waited for the prisoners to crack, but sometimes the Americans just did it themselves.

Was this under orders?

There was certainly always an officer ordering it to be done, sometimes verbally, sometimes with shrugs and other such gestures.

Had the sergeant ever tortured anyone himself?

He had.

The sergeant was thin with a little toothbrush of a mustache. He shifted uneasily in his seat.

Yes, he had, he repeated. Usually with an army field telephone. The phone had a hand-cranked electric generator. He would disconnect the phone and run wires straight from the two poles of the generator to the prisoner's testicles. Then he'd crank the handle. When the juice hit him, the prisoner usually screamed and flopped around like a fish on a line.

Did the men in the sergeant's unit have a saying about this procedure?

Yes, they did.

And what was that?

"Dial him up," the sergeant said, "and he rings."

The judge ruled that the sergeant's testimony was irrelevant and barred it from court.

My second and last direct encounter happened in early 1975 in Saigon, some three months before the city fell. In those days you could sit in the downtown hotel roof gardens and watch the artillery flashes in the surrounding countryside. I took the bus to a Catholic working-class district a half an hour or so from my hotel. At a neighborhood church the priest introduced me to Miss Binh.

Miss Binh had been released by the government six months earlier after more than five years in the infamous "tiger cages" on Con Son Island, where none of the cells was large enough for even the tiny Miss Binh to stand up. The prisoners who survived Con Son did so by capturing bugs to eat and catching raindrops in a cup or occasionally drinking their own urine. Miss Binh had been a teenager when she was arrested. We sat in chairs arranged in the shade on the church's bare dirt grounds.

First, she said, the police questioned her about the church youth group that had staged a demonstration asking the government to settle the war in negotiations with the National Liberation Front. Then they took her to a room in a building somewhere near the Presidential Palace, though she was never sure exactly where it was. All the people around her were Vietnamese in uniforms. They hung her by her arms for several days before they asked her more questions. Then they beat her with cane sticks and burned her with cigarettes. Eventually she was strapped to a table with electrodes attached to her nipples and the lips of her vagina. When they turned the electricity on, she wished she could die. Her interrogators stopped at intervals, and when they left the room she could hear them speaking English with someone in the hallway. Once they left the door ajar by accident, and she saw a tall white man wearing an aqua-colored polyester shirt covered with red flowers.

When Miss Binh's eyes met his, the American in the cheap shirt averted his glance, took a deep hit on his cigarette, and slammed the door shut.

In our war we did things Americans had never allowed themselves to do before.

The Phoenix program was at the top of that list of firsts. The program was named for a mythical omnipresent bird of prey called *phung hoang* in Vietnamese. Phung Hoang was the first comprehensive system of rump legality, kidnapping, torture, and assassination ever designed and run by the United States. Its architect and administrator was the Central Intelligence Agency, using the Agency for International Development as a front; Air America, the CIA's wholly

owned airline, as a prop; and a large batch of pseudo-
nyms, including Combined Study Group, Pacification
Security Coordination Division, and Political and
Economic Section, all headquartered in our embassy
in Saigon. Commenced in late 1967, the Agency's
Phung Hoang lasted in one form or another until the
very end of the war.

Like much of the war, it began as some Washington
whiz kid's brainchild. The issue was how to attack the
Vietcong and, specifically, what the analysts called its
infrastructure. The National Liberation Front ran an
entire parallel system of governance throughout much
of both the countryside they controlled and that sup-
posedly controlled by the Republic of Vietnam. Those
who administered that NLF system, who recruited
new guerrillas, collected taxes, and ran the logistics of
their fight, were considered Vietcong Infrastructure or
VCI. Previous pacification programs had failed to root
out much VCI, and the grunts' search-and-destroy
sweeps had no apparent impact either. Phung Hoang
was the solution the CIA came up with.

Like all American operations, it had a considerable
infrastructure of its own. Working through AID, the
Phung Hoang administrators constructed forty-four
provincial interrogation centers and 242 district posts.
These were specifically charged with enforcing a body
of South Vietnamese law that included the crime of
"pro-communist neutralism," violators to be tried by

military and police tribunals from which there was no appeal. Pro-communist neutralism was defined as neutralism that included any criticism whatsoever of the government or its war effort. It was a blanket under which virtually anyone could be arrested for whatever they chose to charge them with.

To carry out this enforcement at ground level, the CIA counted primarily on its Provincial Reconnaissance Units or PRUs, a five-thousand-man group of Vietnamese mercenaries whom the Agency paid in a straight black-bag operation. On PRU payday Air America choppers landed with agents who doled everyone's cash out of a big box, one man at a time. In at least some provinces, bonuses were paid for dead VC, but that had to include proof of the kill. The PRUs were supplemented by the Special Branch, a seventeen-thousand-man police force, and the fifteen-thousand-man National Police Field Force, a paramilitary unit. Both of these were also paid by the CIA. In the field Phung Hoang was supervised by CIA agents in the more urban areas and U.S. military officers out in the sticks, usually military intelligence, Green Berets, or Navy SEALs acting under Agency orders. The SEALs also did some direct work for Phung Hoang on clandestine missions.

The Phung Hoang process began with a network of informants of all varieties feeding back through the PRUs or directly to the American case officers. They produced names of suspected VC or their allies. There were no safeguards in the process, and at the very least it made the PRU a force to be feared and bought off if at all possible. Being able to put someone on the list was an extraordinary power. Those names were fed into a computer at the Saigon embassy, and monthly "neutralization" quotas were set for each province. They were, of course, to be filled from the list.

Neutralization was another one of those verbal tricks this war seemed to specialize in: covering a host of sins with a word that made them sound like a procedure scheduled every six months in the life of a hydraulic transmission. In the case of Phung Hoang, neutralization translated into two principal activities.

The first began when the people whose names were on the list were dragged into the interrogation center and tortured, a task the PRUs took to with a certain relish. One American agent working Phung Hoang out in the field complained to his Saigon superiors that he was being housed right next to the interrogation center and it was impossible to sleep because of the screaming coming from the building twenty-four hours a day. The saying among the PRUs was "If they are innocent, beat them until they're guilty." Many people whose names were on the list died under torture, but those who survived or confessed were hauled in front of a Pacification Security Committee, a tribunal of police and military officers who handed out sentences for pro-communist neutralism and the like. The sentenced prisoners were then moved to one of thirty-eight regional "reeducation camps," occasionally by Air America charter flights.

The most famous of these prison complexes was on Con Son Island in the South China Sea, where Miss Binh had spent so much of her young life. The tiger cages there were cells dug into the ground, five feet wide by nine feet long by five feet deep, with a grate of iron bars for a ceiling. Each cell held a half dozen people. Often raw lime was thrown into the pits, eventually blinding a number of prisoners. Elsewhere on the island were a series of barbed-wire enclosures called cow cages. The inmates in these were kept constantly shackled. After the war those prisoners were withered, unable to stand or walk, moving themselves around on little wheeled pallets. All told, Phung Hoang processed perhaps 200,000 people or more through its provincial interrogation centers and on down the line. No real numbers have ever been made public by those who know.

Phung Hoang's other principal activity occurred without involving the interrogation centers at all. In this instance, the names on the list were simply killed. The PRU assassins usually worked with American automatic pistols fitted with silencers. They liked to sneak into their targets' residences in the middle of the night and put them away quickly as they slept. When the kill was in territory controlled by the VC, it became a clandestine military operation. The Navy SEALs did a lot of them. They liked to kill with knives. Sometimes the PRU would send teams into similar areas, set up ambushes, and shoot whoever chanced by, all of whom were, of course, presumed to be VC and hence sources of extra income. One American army officer visiting a Phung Hoang compound remembered dinner being interrupted by a PRU noncom come to cash in a half dozen sets of human ears, the proof required for a bonus.

Other than their computer printouts, the Americans often had little idea who their PRUs were out there killing or what those dead amounted to, but they knew the killing was going on and they knew the dead included old women and children. The CIA's own figures accounted for some 21,000 dead through 1971. Later printed estimates have gone as high as 40,000 killed before the American evacuation. From January 1973 on, the American military officers were out of the Phung Hoang chain of command, but the CIA wasn't, and it continued the program until forced to pack up its PRUs and run in April 1975. There are no statistics at all for those last two years, but neutralization continued apace until the very end.

When asked by a Senate committee for an explanation of what his Agency had been doing, the CIA director who had spearheaded Phung Hoang denied that there had been any assassinations and maintained that all of the more than twenty thousand dead suspects had been killed while resisting arrest.

The lying, of course, was standard operating procedure. Everybody up and down the chain of command did it, starting with the commander in chief and ending with the last in the long line of conscripts at his beck and call. There was a way things were supposed to be, which they never were, but everybody who had anything official to say said they were anyway, over and over again. The war proceeded with the warp and woof of one self-serving deception after another. And what wasn't altered or obfuscated was simply concealed behind the relentless public-relations onslaught: some of us told the rest of us whatever we wanted to hear, and, since it was safer to be lied to, most of us accepted it, stared away at every opportunity, and looked askance at those of us who did not. All that lying may have cost us almost as much as the senseless brutality that was the war's signature trait.

The first effect of the lying was to devalue the entire information process. Accurate information was evidence, and concealing evidence from the rest of us was the task to which we put much of our official intelligence. All the organizational channels we had for knowing exactly what was going on were clogged by the need to generate enough verbiage to paper over the war's always dismal prospects, not to mention the ugliness of its product. So we just lied, fooling ourselves and making decisions out of whole cloth or thin air or both. That kind of blindness cost us pieces of our soul, not to mention the prolonged agony of our soldiers. Nobody wanted to hear about what was really going on, so nobody did except those who were prepared to bail out altogether and those for whom it was already too late.

The absence of real information in the public domain also threw our democracy out of kilter and created a circumstance in which the war bureaucracy always had the upper hand. Already blessed with the political cover provided by young men out in harm's way on the country's behalf, Robert S. McNamara, Henry Kissinger, and their like could also take constant and largely unchallenged refuge in their presumed "superior" knowledge of events, even though their cited knowledge turned out to be largely sham they had manufactured themselves. As a consequence of this imbalance, the war carried on with an enormous inertia that was almost impossible to reverse once it became apparent that we had no other remaining options. Those in power had seized the license to make whatever representations they wanted, with or without a basis in fact, and then imprint them with all the credibility of the institutions forged over almost two hundred years of struggling democracy, leveraging the very stuffings of our nation in the hope of maintaining a policy with little else to recommend it.

That was, of course, an unmitigated disaster. It was also a practice that was next to impossible to curb once in common circulation. Eventually lying became habit enough that even its practitioners could no longer distinguish where the lie left off and truth began. Everything became spin. Prevarication was soon endemic to the political process, as addicting as it was useful, and most of America's top shelf has been strung out on it ever since.

The highest official I personally heard lie during the war was Secretary of State Dean Rusk, at the State Department in the beginning of 1967. Rusk met with a delegation of student body presidents who had signed a mild statement questioning the war. I was the "radical" of the group. I had a beard and had been forced to borrow a tie for our appearance since I hadn't thought to bring one with me when I flew east. I had already been down to Fresno for my preinduction physical, and Local Board No. 71 had recently classified me 1-A, fit to serve. I remember the State Department had the thickest carpet I had ever walked across and the quietest typewriters. The hallways were like tombs.

Rusk had a round face with liver spots across his nose, and ears that stuck out like teacup handles. All the student body presidents sat around a very long table, and he stood at its head, lecturing us about

"Communist aggression." The American resistance to it in Vietnam had "turned the corner," he said. The countryside would soon be completely pacified, and the enemy was experiencing "great difficulties." The president wanted peace as much as or more than anyone in this room. The problem was North Vietnamese aggression.

With a droning exclamation, the secretary of state then announced once again that the United States had collected information for the last five years documenting the supply of weapons from the North Vietnamese to the Vietcong. Then he paused to look at his notes.

I interrupted the silence. I couldn't tolerate just sitting and listening to it anymore. There were too many people dying to stay quiet.

We weren't supplying any weapons to the area ourselves, were we? I asked.

Rusk looked up at me over his glasses.

My line was longer on sarcasm than was usual for me, but I wanted it clear what I thought of the hypocrisy of condemning the other side for doing as we were doing ourselves.

Rusk paused only long enough for the glance in my direction, then resumed where he'd left off. The only response to my interruption was from a State Department security officer, who moved over, stood directly behind me, and remained there until the secretary of state cut off his lecture and returned to work.

.   .   .

The high point of Dean Rusk's statecraft was a State Department "white paper," *Aggression from the North,* released with great fanfare in February 1965. "South Vietnam is fighting for its life against a brutal campaign of terror and armed attack," it began, "inspired, directed, supplied, and controlled by the Communist regime in Hanoi." In those days, of course, there were only American "advisers" in Vietnam, though casualties among them were mounting, and Washington was still fishing for a public reason sufficient to explain sending something significantly more substantial.

Rusk's white paper was as close to such a reason as we ever got. It was short, some fifteen printed pages, and written in five sections, sandwiched by an introduction and conclusion. The first four sections— "Hanoi Supplies the Key Personnel for the Armed Aggression Against South Vietnam," "Hanoi Supplies Weapons, Ammunition, and Other War Materiel to Its Forces in the South," "North Vietnam: Base for Conquest of the South," and "Organization, Direction, Command, and Control of the Attack on South Vietnam Are Centered in Hanoi"—made the case that the National Liberation Front, now waging guerrilla warfare everywhere south of the seventeenth parallel, was not an indigenous uprising but an invasion not unlike when North Korea attacked South. The fifth section, "A Brief History of Hanoi's Campaign of Aggression

Against South Vietnam," failed to mention either that the Geneva Accords of 1954 had stipulated free elections and a speedy transition to a unified Vietnam or that the same agreements specifically stipulated that the United States' military mission was limited to 684 men, a command that now stood at some 23,000. Rather this "brief history" argued that the reason for Hanoi's "aggression" was the "economic miracle" of South Vietnam and its contrast to North Vietnam's own economic failures.

"The record is conclusive," the white paper stated. "The people of South Vietnam have chosen to resist this threat. At their request, the United States has taken its place beside them in their defensive struggle. The United States seeks no territory . . . but we have learned the meaning of aggression elsewhere in the post-war world and we have met it. . . . The United States . . . will not abandon friends who want to remain free. It will do what must be done to help them. The choice now between peace and continued and increasingly destructive conflict is one for the authorities in Hanoi to make."

The actual evidence supporting the white paper's conclusions was sprinkled here and there in the text and augmented by a series of appendices distributed far less widely than the white paper itself. Even under the limited scrutiny of the day, this evidentiary underpinning looked shaky at best.

One appendix provided an elaborate table covering the years 1959 to 1964 and showing the number of "confirmed" North Vietnamese infiltrators per year. *Confirmed* was defined as "based on information . . . from at least two independent sources"—that was all. The total infiltration over that entire period was recorded as 19,550. The white paper ignored the fact that this figure, even if accurate, was some 25 percent less than the number of troops we had assigned to Vietnam over the same period and went on to claim specifically that, of the more than 7,000 "Vietcong who are known to have entered the South in 1964," as many as 75 percent were natives of the North. The proof was provided by a collection of "individual case histories of North Vietnamese soldiers" in which all nine individuals were actually from the South; by a list of five captured infiltrators, one of whom was from the South; and by an appendix filled with the case histories of nine Vietcong, seven of whom were born in the South as well. In total the white paper was able to cite only six actual captured natives of North Vietnam for the five-year period it chose to study.

Its proof of the alleged logistical support was comparable: the white paper cited types of Communist-bloc weapons then being captured by ARVN, like the Chinese 7.62-mm assault rifle, but it did not cite numbers, primarily because the numbers were not that impressive. According to the Pentagon's statistics, in the previous eighteen months, our side had lost some 15,000 weapons to the other side and seized some 7,500 weapons from them. Of those 7,500 weapons, 179 had been manufactured in the Communist bloc, a quantity insufficient to outfit even one battalion and not quite 3 percent of the total weapons seizure. So, with only tepid statistics with which to make its case, the white paper leaned heavily on "dramatic new proof... exposed just as this report was being completed."

This proof was the February 16 discovery of a hundred-ton Communist arms transport in South Vietnamese waters. According to the white paper, it was attacked by a flight of South Vietnamese air force planes and sunk in shallow water. When the wreck was searched, the bodies of several dead Vietcong were found, along with a January 23 Haiphong newspaper in the ship's cabin and a hold full of "thousands of weapons and more than a million rounds of ammunition . . . almost all of Communist origin." The white paper text devoted half a page to listing everything that had been discovered, including "500 pounds of medical supplies (with labels from North Vietnam, Communist China, Czechoslovakia, East Germany, Soviet Union and other sources)." The ship itself was tiny as transports go, about one seventy-fifth the size of a standard World War II Liberty ship, and the cargo of little military significance, but the seizure was considered remarkable at the time, principally because it was so rare. The South Vietnamese navy searched twelve thousand coastal vessels a month, and this was the first time they had ever come across an arms cargo of even this modest size.

The mystery of this boat was not solved until 1982, when a former Asia specialist and handler in the CIA's top-secret Directorate for Operations revealed that the Agency had collected the arms, loaded the boat, faked the firefight, sunk the boat, and arranged for news of the find to leak into the press. At the same time, according to the former handler, the Agency had been counterfeiting a Vietcong postage stamp that showed VC firing at an American helicopter. The stamp was a multicolor job requiring a sophisticated printing press of a type that was unavailable in NLF liberated territory but that could be found in North Vietnam; hence the stamp was further "proof" of Hanoi's role.

The rest, of course, is old news. A week after Dean Rusk's white paper was released, *Life* magazine, America's largest-circulation weekly, ran a photo of the CIA's bogus postage stamp on its cover, billing it as more evidence that the Vietcong were a North Vietnamese front, just like the secretary of state said. A week after that, the Ninth Marine Expeditionary Brigade landed at Da Nang and became our first combat unit dispatched to the tall grass. It would not be alone for long.

. . .

By the last few years of the war, the government became so used to lying to the rest of us that it was even prepared to go to court to defend its right to do so. That episode has come down through history tagged as the Pentagon Papers incident. The papers in question were the final results of an enormous top-secret study of the history of our Vietnam involvement, commissioned by Secretary of Defense Robert McNamara and delivered by a private contractor, the Rand Corporation, during the Nixon administration. One of those involved in the effort was a young former Marine Corps officer and National Security Council whiz kid, Daniel Ellsberg. Ellsberg eventually began having second thoughts about what was going on and took a copy of the study, which he had purloined from Rand when he had worked there, and asked *The New York Times* to print it.

Ellsberg and I met after a fashion during the months leading up to his revelations. I was in the penitentiary at the time, on the Texas–New Mexico border, living in a cell on C Block, unloading boxcars all day and playing on the prison basketball team. I was one of a half dozen draft resisters among the institution's six hundred or so inmates. Randy, one of the others, had somehow met Ellsberg shortly before his own incarceration, and Ellsberg visited him several times while he was out on the Texas–New Mexico border with the rest of us. Randy came back from the visiting yard with stories about this guy who'd been working on secret stuff for the Rand Corporation and was now trying to decide whether to take it public and engage in his own version of throwing himself on the cogs of the machine. When Ellsberg eventually did, the Pentagon Papers, as the *Times* dubbed them, became the biggest newspaper story of the war, but none of us listening to Randy's stories had any idea it would amount to something of such a dimension. Decisions about whether to end collusion with the war had been a staple in our lives for years, and we tended to take them for granted.

The study Ellsberg eventually revealed was actually long and dry and remarkable only for how much at variance it was with the official version of events. It was classified secret, but it included no revelations that might aid the enemy. The only revelations were for the home front. According to the Pentagon Papers, our government had known for years that the National Liberation Front had a wide indigenous base of support, that the government of the Republic of Vietnam had an extremely narrow one, that our government's entire public characterization of events was at odds with its private knowledge, and that all the government's own regional experts had been calling the war at best confused for some time.

When the *Times* moved to print its excerpts from Ellsberg's documents, the Nixon administration went to court in an attempt to bar their publication, treating the information as a potential military secret. The federal government also prosecuted Ellsberg for having stolen the papers, treating him as a perpetrator of low-grade espionage. The courts refused to restrain the *Times* and eventually dismissed charges against Ellsberg after a lengthy and expensive trial, largely because it was revealed that a clandestine Nixon administration task force had burglarized Ellsberg's psychiatrist's office in search of evidence with which to discredit him.

By then the war was stumbling into its final chapters, and official fiction had long since become a fixture in American life.

The Tonkin Gulf Resolution, which first gave the war legal footing, was a classic example of the abuse of our trust. It was passed by Congress at the request of President Lyndon Baines Johnson after an alleged attack on the American warships *Maddox* and *Turner Joy* by North Vietnamese patrol boats in the South China Sea on August 4, 1964.

First, the official version:

The *Maddox* and *Turner Joy* were cruising in international waters while the *Maddox* collected electronic information and intercepted radio signals. At the time North Vietnam and the United States were not yet involved in open hostilities, and the *Maddox*'s new electronic center was under the direct authority of the top-secret National Security Agency. On the night of August 2, the *Maddox*'s radar tracked several North Vietnamese PT boats advancing through coastal waters. The *Maddox*'s captain interpreted the sortie as an imminent attack and scattered it with his radar-guided battery from a range of ten miles. The *Turner Joy* was dispatched the next day to protect the *Maddox* in any future encounters.

On the morning of August 4, the NSA man running the *Maddox*'s electronic monitoring equipment reported that his black boxes had picked up radio traffic indicating the North Vietnamese were going to muster another PT boat attack. That evening the fog was thick and not much of anything was visible, except, of course, to the *Maddox*'s radar and sonar. Those instruments soon began reading another North Vietnamese advance. The *Maddox* increased speed to its maximum thirty knots and began zigzagging. At 9:52 P.M., the captain reported that he was under torpedo attack, and over the next two hours the *Maddox*'s sonar machinery discerned between twenty-two and thirty torpedoes fired in its direction, though there was never a visual sighting of boats or torpedoes, by either the warships or the navy planes dispatched from two nearby aircraft carriers. The *Turner Joy* nonetheless claimed to have sunk one North Vietnamese ship and damaged another on the basis of its interpretations of radar blips.

Within hours President Johnson preempted programming on all three national television networks to denounce the unprovoked attack and announce that, as he spoke, bombers from the American carrier force in the South China Sea were retaliating against targets in North Vietnam. He would soon be going to Congress, he said, for authorization "to repel any armed attack against the forces of the United States and to prevent further aggression." The next day public-opinion polls, in which Johnson's Vietnam policy had been registering 58 percent disapproval, flipped over to 72 percent support. Two days after that, the House of Representatives passed the Tonkin Gulf Resolution 416–0, the Senate, 88–2. Henceforth it would be just a matter of passing larger and larger budgets.

What really happened to the *Maddox* on the evening of August 4, 1964, hardly seems worth it. While the *Maddox* may have been in international waters, other American vessels were simultaneously operating closer to shore. Since July 30 American boats had been ferrying clandestine groups of Republic of Vietnam and American commandos inside the twenty-mile limit to conduct sabotage operations against North Vietnamese shore defenses. The latest attack had been staged on the evening of August 3. The threatening radio intercept on the morning of August 4 was in fact an order to "make ready for military operations" sent to two North Vietnamese boats, neither of which was capable of firing torpedoes. As soon as Johnson learned of the radio intercept, twelve hours before there had been any reports of an attack, he told McNamara to destroy those boats and the harbor they came out of. When reports of the attack were received, planning for the response had already begun. The president quickly informed the admiral in charge that he wanted a bombing mission against North Vietnam.

Out on the South China Sea, however, the attack on the *Maddox* had already lost credibility. The dispatched navy fighters dropped flares, flew at wave-top level, searched the whole map grid around the *Maddox* both visually and with radar, and never saw a thing. As one of the pilots put it, "no boat wakes, no ricochets off boats, no boat gunfire, no torpedo wakes—nothing but black sea and American firepower." The commander of the flight reported upon his return that nothing whatsoever had happened out there and that the attack was a figment of someone's imagination. By then even the *Maddox*'s captain was having his doubts. They began when the sonar room reported close to thirty torpedo firings, a finding that eventually caused laughter in the officers' boardroom. It was a well-known piece of naval intelligence that North Vietnam owned only twenty-four torpedoes in its entire arsenal. After a war council the captain also concluded that the sightings might very well have been either inconsequential radar blips or reflections of the sonar off the zigzagging ship's own rudder. He wired the chain of command that the reported contacts appeared "doubtful" and suggested "complete evaluation before any further action taken." In fact, there was no sure evidence that any North Vietnamese vessel had even been in the *Maddox*'s vicinity on the evening of August 4.

The admiral told the president, but the president only reminded the admiral that he wanted a bombing flight mustered by 11:15 P.M. eastern daylight time. Any later and the president's speech would miss the last window into prime time. The navy never did figure out whether the North Vietnamese attack actually happened. As airtime approached, the admiral told the president that technical difficulties were going to prevent the task force from getting its bombers in the air before the television deadline and asked him to hold his announcement so the targets wouldn't have advance warning. Johnson gave his speech anyway. One navy pilot was killed in the subsequent raid, and another was shot down and captured. The president's political advisers were later frank about the fact that Johnson, in the midst of an election campaign, had long since decided he had to make some show of military force to blunt any criticism from the right. The Gulf of Tonkin was it.

Having used an incident that never happened to start a war that he could never stop, Lyndon Johnson swept the November 1964 election as a peace candidate and served another four years as president. By the time his new term was up, some 540,000 American soldiers were stationed in Vietnam and he was being hounded out of politics to chants of "Hey, hey, LBJ, how many kids did you kill today?" It was said that he kept a copy of the Tonkin Gulf Resolution in his pocket and, in private conversations, was given to pulling it out for spontaneous oral readings when anyone raised questions about his authority to wage the war. That sounds like Johnson.

I remember him well: not one thing he ever told us in his entire five years as president of the United States was half as real as the vacant faces on the dead boys who were soon being sacked up and shipped home in bulk.

There is, of course, no redeeming those wasted lives. And that finality may be the hardest part of our memory. "Ain't no way to satisfy the dead" is the way Tommy put it.

Tommy was friends with J.C., a New Mexico smuggler who was a buddy of mine from prison. Tommy'd been at Hamburger Hill in 1969 with the 173rd Airborne when what remained of his outfit refused to obey an order to return to battle. The order was changed, and Tommy just finished up his twelve-month tour and got out. The war had been over for more than a year by the time we talked. The three of us were sitting in Taos, New Mexico, at a table in the shade outside J.C.'s tiny pool hall. The afternoon was dusty, and there was a cottonwood full of magpies nearby.

"Ain't no way to satisfy the dead," Tommy said, talking about the ghosts the 173rd had left behind in the Central Highlands.

He paused, letting the sounds from the cottonwood drift through. "The dead know what they need," he said, "but we can't give it to 'em."

I let the statement sit a bit before finally asking what Tommy thought all those lost boys were needing.

He stared at me and then at the mountains behind my shoulder. "A reason," he said.

Those two words hung in the air for a long while. Then Tommy began to chuckle and the chuckle turned into a laugh and after a bit the laugh stopped.

Tommy shook his head. Tears were running down his face.

"Ain't that a bitch?" he said. "Ain't that a fuckin' bitch?"

7

WITH MY BUDDHIST ASPIRATIONS, I like to think I believe in forgiveness and redemption, but there are parts of the war I remember that challenge my faith: people and episodes about which I still lose my balance, hatreds that have lingered and of which I still cannot let go. Of these, Robert McNamara and Henry Kissinger are perhaps the archetypes.

McNamara recently returned to the newspaper headlines with the release of a memoir in which he became the highest-ranking American official to admit that the war should never have been fought. His book revealed that as early as 1966, barely a year into the pattern of escalation that would eventually put over half a million Americans in Vietnam, he and others among the inner circles of the Johnson administration already considered the effort an unwinnable waste of lives and matériel. The war, of course, lasted another nine years. In his book McNamara explained his twenty-nine-year public silence about his conclusions as the necessary loyalty of a cabinet officer to his president.

McNamara's coming out was tumultuous for everyone and consumed a couple weeks' worth of national talk shows and front-page news stories. It was a big moment for me as well: I had once distributed leaflets identifying McNamara as the man who made the war machine run, and his picture had hung on the wall of the induction-center office where I was evaluated as fit to serve. That he finally admitted to the bankruptcy of the assault he'd administered for Lyndon Johnson was touching to me as well as gratifying. I instantly recognized how far he'd come to say such things, and I can only commend the movement.

The rest of me, however, still screams out, *Why on earth did you wait so long?* If Robert S. McNamara had spoken up in 1966 instead of 1995, the landscape in the American wake would look altogether different than it does. Hundreds of thousands of ghosts would still be alive, and a whole generation's worth of pain would be stored away, largely unspent. We deserved far better from the man charged with the sacred trust of sending the nation's children in harm's way. The eternal bottom line is unequivocal: a lot more people died after Robert McNamara decided their lives were being wasted than before, and he never said so much as a word to warn them. I am glad he finally told us, but there is nothing he could say now that would let him escape the obvious moral arithmetic. I believe in forgiveness and redemption, and I know both must be a part of any reckoning we engage in, but it is still hard for me to allow the possibility that Robert S. McNamara's slate will ever be clean.

At the time McNamara claimed he was acting the dove in Johnson's cabinet, he certainly did not seem that way from the outside. With the war building every day and the country in hot pursuit of a light at the end of its ever-lengthening tunnel, McNamara was the living symbol of an attitude that still makes me shudder. He was an industrial whiz kid, one of the saviors of the Ford Motor Company, a missionary for a genre of materialist accountancy that everyone considered "modern" and that he was commissioned to bring to the mightiest military in the world. He began his stay at Defense as just the man to enforce efficiency on the department's uniformed bureaucrats and ended it as the architect of a machine that manufactured corpses, eventually to the tune of thousands a week.

His department brought a particular style to their task.

I remember it as the Plastic Fragmentation Bomb System — named, of course, after a notorious weapon developed by the McNamaraized Pentagon. As the massive use of airpower rapidly became a central tenet of American strategy in Vietnam, our military planners had few enemy industrial or war mobilization centers to target, so the target became the population itself. The issue was how to maximize the efficiency of that effort and create the most significant possible drag on the enemy's resources. That led to a study concluding that every enemy killed in the bombardment would require the attention of one and a half others in the immediate aftermath of the attack. The same enemy seriously wounded would require the attention of five. That led to widespread use of the fragmentation bomb: about the size of a guava, made of steel, stuffed with explosives, and dropped by the hundreds in long canisters that opened up during their descent, spreading smaller bombs over a wide range. The smaller bombs were set to trigger at about ten feet off the ground, exploding into thousands of flying razor-sharp metal fragments, angled to reach those hiding in holes as well as those aboveground. The result was an increasing number of wounded, who would each require the efforts of five people to help rather than one and a half. Then some bright young boy in the Pentagon added a last detail to the package: why not manufacture the smaller bombs out of plastic? That way the wounds would not only be serious and plentiful but also relatively untreatable since the fragments that would lodge in the wounded could not be located with an X-ray machine. The unrelieved suffering thus induced would in turn yield an even greater drain on the enemy's resources, maximizing the returns on the American bombardment.

And so it was in the impeccable, if hideous, logic of an efficient Department of Defense. And its secretary, Robert S. McNamara, definitely has more to account for than most.

I first began hearing rumors that McNamara was having trouble living with that debt some ten years ago from other members of the national press corps. People who knew him around Washington, D.C., where he conducted the business of the World Bank, said he didn't sleep well and sometimes had nightmares. When he finally addressed the issue in his book, he admitted to crying easily and always coming slightly unglued when he visited the capital's Vietnam Memorial. I suspect writing it down on paper has given him some relief, though I'm still not sure that I'm glad about that.

Our paths crossed briefly when his book was rocketing to the top of *The New York Times* best-seller list. Several days earlier the *Times* had taken him to task on the editorial page, saying, "His regret cannot be huge enough to balance the books of our dead soldiers. . . . We are still living in the wreckage created by the Cabinet on which Mr. McNamara served." I was in New York at the time, visiting my publisher, and so was he. My editor urged me to meet McNamara, and eventually I was ushered into a conference room where the former secretary of defense, all by himself, was signing a huge pile of books to be distributed to the house's employees. McNamara's son had been at Stanford in the years immediately after I'd been there, so we talked about the school during the sixties, a safe enough subject. Then it was clearly time for me to leave. The secretary had other fish to fry.

First, however, he insisted on inscribing a copy of his book: "To David," he wrote, "an honorable man. With admiration, Robert S. McNamara."

In the months since, I have showed my autographed copy to several friends from the old days, and we have always laughed, shaking our heads in amazement that I should end up with such a relic from such a man.

When I look at that inscription by myself, however, I don't laugh. Rather I am full of endless puzzlement. If Robert S. McNamara indeed feels that way, I cannot begin to fathom how he manages to live with himself. Were I he, I suspect I would have blown my brains out years ago.

Henry Kissinger came relatively late to the tall grass, first as Richard Nixon's national security adviser and then as his secretary of state, but everyone I know who tried to stop the war has a special place in memory for him. We spoke often in those days of "them" and knew exactly who we meant. By the same token, Kissinger was "him." And while a number of attitudes toward them have mellowed over time, no one I know from the old days has lost the venom for him.

Nancy was typical. She'd been a housewife before she became an antiwar organizer. She made the switch one day on the tarmac at Washington's old National Airport. Back then planes were still boarded from stairs wheeled onto the runway. Nancy was waiting for the previous flight to empty so her flight could board. Standing next to her was a mother waiting for her soldier son to disembark. When he reached the top of the stairs, he had two crutches and a stump for a left leg. The mother fainted dead away, and within hours, Nancy had decided to begin organizing against the war.

We got on the subject of Kissinger one afternoon after she'd been through a whole new life as a Senate aide and started yet another as a jewelry importer.

"It's amazing," she said. "All those good people dead, and no one has managed to kill that lousy son of a bitch yet."

I knew exactly how she felt.

There was just something about Henry Kissinger. He certainly brought out the worst in me. Just thinking about him drove me up the wall. Lacey often poked fun at how unbalanced I became when Kissinger's name came up, and she was right on the mark. Her observation led me to an informal private dissection of the hatred so many of us retained for the man and how personally we took him. Using myself as a case study, I have thus far isolated two elements to this mild dementia.

The first was a matter of image. Kissinger seemed so unequivocal about his assumption that the rest of us were just chips in the poker game he and his boss were playing out in the ozone with the Russians and the Chinese. To us he appeared smug about it. Even over the evening news it seemed obvious that Henry was more important to Henry than anybody else. We were convinced he knew the war was a wasted enterprise when he first came on the national security watch, but he was more interested in playing the game. Superpower appearances had to be upheld, whatever the cost. There was no pretense of idealism in him. At least his boss had the human touch of an ideology. Henry brokered only power itself. And he did so with the appearance of phenomenal arrogance. He dealt in geopolitical postures and national interests, which he apparently considered unaccountable for the pain they induced. As far as I was concerned, an awful lot of people died as a consequence, and I'm not sure he's ever noticed.

The second element in my lingering anger is the Christmas bombing of 1972. Again, though, I have to admit that I still bring a lot of my own history to the subject. That fall in 1972 had been just plain ugly. I had finally been freed from the authority of the U.S. Board of Parole, but I was burned out, the antiwar movement was exhausted, Richard Nixon was on his way to an overwhelming reelection, and everyone knew we were going to negotiate our way out of the war any week now. But Kissinger and Nixon couldn't get the deal they wanted from the other side, so the possibility just dangled out there, tortuously close after so many years. In Vietnam the most widely discussed topics were the estimated rates of heroin addiction and officer assassination among the troops. Everybody knew the war was coming to no good end, and no one wanted to die in the last throes of our national embarrassment.

Then, a little more than two weeks before the presidential elections, Kissinger announced that he and the North Vietnamese had cut a deal at secret meetings in Paris and peace was at hand. This, it turned out, ceased to be true almost from the moment he said it. The deal that had been cut was for American withdrawal under "honorable" conditions that allowed our South Vietnamese surrogate, headed by General Nguyen Van Thieu, to remain in place for an undefined interval sufficient to cover American sensibilities about getting out. It was a superpower shadow play to Henry, but to Thieu it smacked of sellout, and the general did his best to sabotage the understanding. At that point Kissinger backed out of the deal and tried to reopen negotiations with the North Vietnamese. Within a week after Nixon's overwhelming reelection, everything had unraveled. On December 13 the North Vietnamese suspended formal negotiations.

According to Nixon, Kissinger was furious at his adversaries. "They're just a bunch of shits," he told the president, "tawdry, filthy shits." He recommended Nixon either intensify the bombing of North Vietnam immediately or wait and resume negotiations again in the new year. Nixon decided to do both.

On December 18, 1972, the United States began its heaviest aerial bombardment of North Vietnam of the entire war. It was dubbed Operation Linebacker II. Over eleven days the Americans flew more than three thousand bomber sorties, dropping some forty thousand tons of explosives on the sixty-mile-long population corridor connecting the cities of Hanoi and its harbor, Haiphong.

The New York Times called the raids "Stone Age barbarism," *The Washington Post*, "savage and senseless." At the time I called Kissinger a lousy, heartless son of a bitch in public, and I swore in private that I would never forgive either him or his boss. And it seems I have kept my pledge, at least until now. A genuine reckoning requires me to open my heart to even Henry Kissinger, but doing so is still a difficult notion for me to fathom.

Operation Linebacker II ended on December 30. The Americans had lost twenty-six aircraft and most of their crews, either killed or captured, and the North Vietnamese had fired every last surface-to-air missile in their arsenal. It was the final significant open American combat operation of the war, and, like its predecessors, Operation Linebacker II fostered much pain and raised considerable havoc, all to no avail.

On January 8, 1973, Henry Kissinger resumed negotiations with the North Vietnamese in Paris, and within twenty-four hours he had agreed to settle for the same deal he'd thrown away in October. On January 27, 1973, the American army began withdrawing, leaving the Republic of Vietnam to carry on by itself.

In the superpower game at which Henry Kissinger was so adept, nations do not have souls. They have interests.

I know no exact definition of what an interest is, but for the game's layperson, I call it a strategic advantage that can be milked for either money or power. And, according to the game, the pursuit of such interests is the prime purpose of all nations, but especially the heavyweights. The only rule is: Anything you can do, you do. We have been one of the major subscribers to the game for most of the twentieth century. Which goes a long way toward explaining how we lost our heart. According to the rules of play, it was not in our interests to keep it.

Witness the Plain of Jars.

The Plain of Jars was an elevated plateau covered with rolling savanna and forests in the heart of Laos's Xieng Khouang province. Elevation 3,500 feet, its climate was mild and its resources rich. Most of Laos's cattle were raised here as well as most of its fruit. Its name came from a number of huge abandoned urns that were the last remainders of some previous civilization about which little was now known. The plain's grasslands turned golden in the dry season and exploded in green once the rain came. It was considered one of the most beautiful locations in Laos. The area was rich in both salt and iron deposits as well as located at the crossroads of an extensive network of trails leading into neighboring Vietnam. Its natural resources and its location had made the plain a hotly contested site throughout the previous thousand years. And once Laos was sucked up in the American onslaught and became our backdoor war, the plain was fought over again. Power in Laos was contested by three armies: one Communist, one pro-American, one neutralist. At the time the American escalation hit its stride in Vietnam, the Communists controlled the Plain of Jars and its some sixty thousand permanent residents.

This posed a unique dilemma for American planners. Our surrogate army was not strong enough to retake the plain, and the front in Laos would not be allowed any American ground troops to do the job in their stead. If America was to hold this place, we would have to do so with airpower alone, an unprecedented military strategy. So the Plain of Jars became the scene of an experiment in warfare as the United States attempted to establish control of a critical piece of geography with no presence on the ground except for a few scouting parties of Hmong. The strategy, according to American planners, was to use air bombardment "to destroy the social and economic infrastructure of the [Communist] held areas." That meant making the Plain of Jars uninhabitable, which is what we did.

It took us five and a half years:

The reconnaissance planes came over first, in the morning as soon as the light was good. They photographed any population groupings they found, marking targets for the dive-bombers. In the beginning most of the bombers were propeller driven, but soon jets played an increasing role. At first there would be perhaps a dozen sorties a day, but after several years it was not unusual for the daily sorties to number in the hundreds. During periods when the bombing of North Vietnam was suspended as part of the diplomatic process, the bombers that had been flying there were often retargeted for the villages on the Plain of Jars. Every day, 365 days a year, for more than five years running, the American arsenal rained on the plain: jellied gasoline, white phosphorus, delayed action, fragmentation, fléchette, and ball-bearing bombs. The phosphorus made the worst wounds, sometimes burning inside the flesh of the wounded for days, emitting a ghastly green glow. The children were the most vulnerable to the aerial onslaught. They were the slowest to adapt to a life of constant hiding and had a knack for going out to play at just the wrong time. Gunships often followed bombardments with strafing runs, firing at anything that moved.

By 1970, a year after the presidency of the United States and stewardship of the war had passed from Lyndon Johnson to Richard Nixon, there were no stationary structures left on the entire highland plateau. Its sixty thousand residents were descendants of people who had lived among its savanna and forests for all of their collective memory, but by 1970 those who were still alive had either fled with the Communists into the escarpment or wandered down to lowland refugee camps. For the first time in tens of centuries, there was no human civilization at all on the Plain of Jars.

The American experiment was a success.

Cambodia was perhaps the war's classic chapter in this heartless game of interests: poor Cambodia, the wretched killing field that started as something close to Shangri-la and ended in the heart of darkness, spawned by the whirlwind, nurtured by the Apocalypse.

Cambodia stayed neutral for the first six years the Americans were in Indochina, relatively untouched by the war. The Cambodian state was balanced under the monarch, Prince Norodom Sihanouk, in a rough coalition that had managed to dodge all the region's major players without significant collisions. The Americans disapproved of neutralists in principle but tolerated Sihanouk and had their hands full elsewhere for most of the decade. The Russians weren't all that excited by neutralists either, but since Sihanouk turned a blind eye to the presence of large bodies of NLF and North Vietnamese troops taking sanctuary in Cambodian border areas, the Russians tolerated him as well. The Chinese backed an obscure guerrilla group called the Khmer Rouge, but not to a great degree, content simply to keep a hand in the action rather than attempt to bring Sihanouk down. The balancing act fell apart when Richard Nixon and Henry Kissinger, bedeviled by their failing war next door, decided that a clear message had to be sent to the Russians and their Vietnamese clients. America would no longer tolerate such an obvious transgression against its interests.

So the Americans got the game rolling when they backed a group of Cambodian generals led by one Lon Nol and overthrew Sihanouk. Sihanouk fled to exile in Beijing and became the public ally of the Khmer Rouge. Shortly afterward the Americans invaded several of the Vietnamese Cambodian sanctuaries at the invitation of Lon Nol's government. On an ongoing basis, though, Lon Nol and his patrons made no pretense of being able to expel the Vietnamese troops. They chose saturation bombing by the Americans instead and focused infantry action on the Khmer Rouge, who were suddenly thrust forward by their alliance with Cambodia's most popular public figure and reinforced with fresh loads of Chinese military hardware. The result was a four-year fight, which Lon Nol lost despite the best efforts of the American air armada. We evacuated our embassy in Phnom Penh just two weeks before we abandoned our embassy in Saigon.

The Khmer Rouge proceeded to take power and kill more than a million Cambodians in one of history's great mass exterminations. That killing stopped only when the Vietnamese invaded in 1979, scattered the Khmer Rouge, and occupied the whole country. The Americans, fearing Vietnamese expansionism and rising Soviet influence in the region, complained to the Russians and then made common diplomatic cause with the Chinese, insisting that the Vietnamese withdraw from Cambodia and that the Khmer Rouge execution squads, now once again allied with the exiled Sihanouk, be given due consideration in the formulation of Cambodia's legitimate government. After almost a decade of postures and negotiations, the

Vietnamese withdrew in favor of a coalition of Sihanouk, the surrogate government established by the Vietnamese, and the Khmer Rouge. Then, after national elections supervised by the United Nations, power was transferred to a neutralist political coalition with Sihanouk as figurehead, backed by the Russians and the Americans. The Khmer Rouge, still backed by the Chinese, removed to the jungle, once again to engage in sporadic guerrilla warfare.

So, almost twenty-five years to the day after the Cambodian chapter of the superpower game opened, we had finally chased our interests in a complete circle and returned to the spot from which we'd first embarked, now cast in the shadow of a long-lost Shangri-la and haunted by more ghosts than anybody could shake a stick at.

The war has clung to me over all the years since its end, but these days I feel less haunted by it than just dogged. It does not populate my sleep with nightmares or my waking hours with flashbacks or cause me to bounce from one wall to another. There are times, however, when the resonance of a moment evokes moments long ago and I am suddenly thrown back into the same spot as the old days: standing apart from the mass, offended by the lies, incredulous that such blind arrogance could hold sway, alienated from the norm and proud of it. The most recent of those episodes came when I turned on my television and tried to watch the funeral of Richard Milhous Nixon, thirty-seventh president of the United States.

By then, of course, I had buried my own share of loved ones and was familiar with the need of those who knew Richard Nixon well to honor their bonds, but it has always seemed to me that public observances have additional standards. In marking those kinds of passings, we also make choices about our own legend and what memory we imprint on our collective identity. I aspire to be charitable in that circumstance and make judgments of others only in light of an honest acceptance of my own numerous shortcomings, but, that said, Richard Milhous Nixon was as evil a man as any who has ever partaken of the apex of American political power. And in all the dreary progression of statements when he was taken home to Yorba Linda and laid to rest, the subject remained completely untouched.

At the time I attributed my dissonance to the collision of my particular sensitivities with America's ongoing blind spot over the war. The war, after all, was at the root of the worst of Nixon's transgressions: from the beginning of his presidency, he had an obsession about the domestic antiwar movement that had unhorsed Lyndon Johnson, shattered the Democratic party, and opened the door to the White House through which he stepped in a masterpiece of political timing. He did not intend to share LBJ's fate, so he passed few opportunities to bridle at the opposition and, while dangling the possibility of a negotiated settlement, escalated the aggressiveness of American military action so no one would underestimate his mettle. More people died on his watch than any other, and he took a particular public pleasure in the devastation he wrought. He liked his adversaries to think of him as crazy and dangerous, so he behaved that way. There was little Richard Nixon considered out of bounds. He was also easily annoyed, and nothing annoyed him more than the assault on his war powers.

When Nixon was facing impeachment, most of the charges considered against him by the House of Representatives had their roots in this annoyance: Nixon's "plumbers" unit was eventually responsible for a host of malfeasances, including the infamous Watergate burglary, but it was formed to respond to the political threat posed by the increasing visibility of organizations of Vietnam veterans now opposed to the war. Among the plumbers' black-bag jobs was the burglary of Daniel Ellsberg's psychiatrist's office. Their surveillances included several prominent antiwar figures, their fronts included a phony "patriotic" veterans' organization. All the while, of course, Nixon kept up his adversarial madness and unleashed an armada that churned its way back and forth across Southeast Asia, extracting the heaviest price we could muster. If

Robert McNamara did more than he can ever answer for, then Richard Nixon was in that position several times over.

None of that perspective made it into the ceremonies publicly marking Nixon's passing. He had been rehabilitated by then: his crimes against the Constitution diminished into distant memory, his crimes against the helpless ten thousand miles away and the rest of us here at home never acknowledged. The Nixon we buried was a statesman and political wise man, a man of letters and sage insight. When those characterizations began rolling toward me out of the television, I turned it off and left it off. I had lived with Richard Nixon in our public life for all of mine, and, no matter how many treaties he signed in how many places, he was to me never more than someone from whom no one in their right mind would buy a used car. His career of public service demeaned all of us, start to finish. And the only chord his passing struck in me was a loss of the familiar. Even I was used to him by the end.

His Senate campaign in my home state had been a landmark of red-baiting hysteria since I first knew there was such a thing as politics. His loss of the presidency to John Kennedy had been a landmark in the public imagination, an almost legendary video triumph of the light and well decorated over the dark and lurking; his loss of the California governor's election two years later, a landmark in greasy bitterness; his rehabilitation for his actual election to the presidency, a landmark in political hype. He defined the worst in our public self. His was the most recognized face in American politics, with its squared-off nose and sandpaper jaw, and he never looked anything but sinister.

His official photograph, needless to say, looked a lot more benign than that. I remember it on the wall of the room into which I was taken to meet with the judge from the parole board. It was a walk out of my cell on C Block, through my cell gate and two locked cellblock doors, down a staircase, past the control center, through two more locked doors, and down a corridor. I sat facing a wide wooden table, and the judge sat across from me. His chair had arms and mine did not. The hearing was being recorded by a reel-to-reel tape machine on the table. Richard Nixon's picture was just over the judge's shoulder, looking straight at me. The judge posed questions and I answered.

If you were drafted for a war to defend Israel, would you still refuse? the judge asked with a kind of chortle in his voice, as though he knew this was a question for which he was sure I had no answer.

I looked over the judge's shoulder at Richard Milhous Nixon and then back to the judge. Nixon had eyes like a raptor, and the judge had eyes like Cream of Wheat.

I told the judge I took my wars one at a time.

He waited for me to continue, and when I didn't he asked if there wasn't something more I wanted to say.

I said I also suspected the government would like to get done with the war they had going before they sent me an invitation to another. "But," I added, motioning with my head toward the picture of Nixon on the jailhouse wall, "who knows? With that motherfucker, anything's possible."

The judge pursed his lips and closed the file in front of him. My hearing was adjourned.

8

THE WAR REVISITS all of us who knew it, each in our own private way.

I first interviewed Sergeant Ron in Santa Monica, out by L.A.'s best beach, in the days when I worked for *Rolling Stone*. Eventually Tom Cruise played Ron in a movie about his life, but back then he was largely unknown to the national media, except as a long-haired paraplegic veteran who'd interrupted the speech of Richard Nixon at the Republican National Convention in 1972. I knew him through my Movement connections. Ron had become a frequent speaker at Southern California antiwar rallies, representing Vietnam Veterans Against the War.

As always, Sergeant Ron was seated in his chair, often resting his elbows on its wheels. His legs dangled like two useless noodles; when he wanted to shift himself, he had to pick them up with his hands and relocate them one at a time. They'd been that way since January 20, 1967. He was a sergeant with the Third Marines then, barely twenty years old but already doing his second tour, working the sand and stumpy pine trees around the Rockpile and the DMZ. He had been born on the Fourth of July, wrestled for Massapequa High, and enlisted, eager to serve his country out where the dust turned boots yellow and brave men proved their mettle.

On January 20, Victor Charlie opened up on Ron's platoon just as it emerged from a village, headed toward the trees. The combat had been heavy all winter, including lots of NVA incoming. This morning the marines scattered when the tree line opened up, and Ron ran forward to muster an assault.

When the big hit finally came, Sergeant Ron was playing John Wayne to the hilt. He'd already been shot through the foot and had been dragging it along and firing from the hip. He eventually dove onto the sand and fired from his stomach until the sand jammed his gun. Then, just as he pushed himself up to see where the rest of his men were, an AK-47 round, rushing at some 3,500 feet per second, entered through the soft meat of his shoulder and collided with his spinal cord. Ron's first thought was that he'd been run over by a train, and he has not been able to feel anything south of his belly button since. Two other marines were killed trying to pull him back from the open ground upon which he'd fallen. Finally a grunt he'd never seen before, and has never seen since, sprinted through machine-gun fire, slung him over his shoulder, and fetched him to safety. A helicopter eventually hauled him to a hospital tent in which everyone around him died and he was expected to do likewise. But he survived against all odds and was shipped home to a New York VA hospital where rats scurried across his chest and nibbled on his now vacant toes.

Ron was still in no mood to forgive anyone.

"The war ain't over," he lamented that day in Santa Monica. "Ask somebody who fought it. The war ain't over until you don't have to live with it anymore."

Over the years lots of war stories have drifted my way. Some kind of karmic magnetism seems to draw them. People who know what I did about the war often feel a certain compulsion to talk to me about what they did back then as well, and I have a compulsion for polite listening, at least up to a point. I am also on the constant lookout for good tales, have reported on issues surrounding the war's leftovers for national publications, and am the only draft resister I know who ever served on the board of a veterans' services organization, so I've managed to accumulate a wide range of stories on all fronts, much the way static electricity accumulates cat hair. Everywhere I wander, they attach. At my Stanford class's twenty-fifth reunion, at least two dozen people whom I did not remember, with no invitation from me, explained at some length their personal tracks through the war. Two dozen whom I did remember did the same.

And so it is for me. Most of these accounts that have managed to lodge in my memory elaborate a dilemma around which some kind of moral calculus was being performed, and as a consequence, over time, I developed my own informal mathematics for assessing the accounts that came my way: a calculation that vectored the actions performed, the risks taken, and the damage done. Somewhere in the relationship of those factors, each of us left a distinct moral fingerprint, or so I assumed.

In idle moments I even cataloged these collected dilemmas into certain rough categories as I listened and, smiling sympathetically, calculated their moral location. In my extremely unscientific sample, easily the most emblematic among these situational phyla were the men who bombed, crewing the giant B-52s that rained tons of high explosives each time they flew. These men are not whom we usually remember first when we recall the tunnel with no light at its end, but their vectors come close to framing the archetype of our much larger mutual dilemma as well their own.

The B-52s' specialty was carpet bombing. Flying from bases in Thailand or Guam, cruising at thirty thousand feet or thereabouts, the bombers navigated to a square marked on a map and released their belly-fuls of high explosives to tumble earthward, saturating the target area with fire, concussion, and white-hot shards of flying metal. Then they made a U-turn and went home. They were an awesome weapons system. The ground churned when they attacked; pocks formed in the crust of the earth itself. The craters they made still occupy patches of the countryside in Viet-nam, filling with rainwater when the monsoons come. The more enterprising survivors have learned to raise fish in the thirty-year-old bomber tracks.

When those tracks were first laid down, people just ran and hid as best they could. Anyone caught in one of those explosions was vaporized. Enemy units trapped under such barrages trembled, even when dug deep into bunkers. Some thought they might go mad from the sound alone or die when the ground shook them to pieces. It was as though some mythic tyran-nosaurus was stomping around on the earth above. Mostly, though, the B-52s caught no enemy units. In postwar assessments their onslaughts proved of little significant military consequence. They did, however, dismember much of the far-off surface over which they flew, make the countryside uninhabitable, and dispatch a procession of millions to the urban areas to escape the ravaging whose onset was signaled only by the whine of jet engines so high in the sky they were out of sight.

For the men who flew at that altitude, however, it was just another day at the office. Their insulation from the consequences of their action was virtually complete. They fought inside a hermetic seal. They never saw where their bombs fell, much less what they did. They also fought in relative safety for almost the entire war. Their planes were used against targets where there was nothing at all to challenge them. It was not until Richard Nixon and Henry Kissinger's Christmas bombings of 1972 that they were sent against defended territory, and in that fight two dozen B-52s were actually lost to the North Vietnamese SAM batteries. Otherwise, their massive barrage was virtually risk-free for the individuals who performed it.

They shared none of the sweaty terror of the grunt holed up outside the perimeter or the door gunner standing to his weapon during the drop into a hot landing zone. These aircrews never used their boots to poke at the dead they left behind or walked through a patch of the smoking pits in which an entire hamlet had disappeared except for the various human chunks strewn about the smoldering underbrush and splintered thatch. Some of these bomber boys even returned to military housing with their wives and children after a mission and spent the evening watching *Gilligan's Island* on military TV. In the bars in Thailand, they would play a game in which someone would yell out a code word like Red Dog or Blaster and everyone had to hit the deck as though an air raid were under way. Last man down bought the next round.

In that extraordinary isolation from both the context and the content of their actions, those bomber boys were like so many of the rest of us. Their dilemma was ours: how to find moral bearings when insulated from the reality we create; how to make sense of ourselves and what we are doing when we never see either, both literally and figuratively; how to justify ourselves in the light of consequences about which no one speaks except in the most mechanical language possible and in which there is little possibility we will personally share; how to discern evil when even the extremes of it have been organized into the most banal packaging.

I've met a lot of people left over from the war, still strung out among those questions, but I have not met a whole lot of answers. And I don't expect to. It's not easy, however we cut it.

There is, however, ample evidence of just how malignant that disproportionate ratio between damage extracted and risk undertaken can be. As surely as deep-sea divers get the bends if they rise too quickly, the moral freeloading involved in exacting the most extreme damage while steadily ignoring the consequences and maintaining the least possible personal exposure makes people rot from their insides out, starting with the heart and going straight to the brain. We saw a lot of it on the home front.

Just how we ought to treat what we'd all been through has, of course, been at issue one way or another ever since the war ground to a halt on the last day of April 1975.

I have participated in that ongoing discussion, though it has been largely of little consequence and nothing if not predictable. Some still maintained a case for the nobility of our enterprise, some quite the contrary, and while those lines occasionally shifted the one constant was that no one disputed the trauma the war left among us.

In its immediate aftermath just about everybody who'd touched or been touched by the war felt burned by it. The draft was disbanded with little in the way of objections, and nobody wanted to hear talk about more intervention, anytime, anywhere. Everyone was sick of being lied to, sick of sending poor boys ten thousand miles from home to kill or be killed. Our trust had been betrayed, our hopes dashed, the fabric of our lives torn end to end. It was hard even to remember those days when the smiling young president stopped by Fresno and the Venerable Thich Quang Duc torched himself at the corner of Phan Dinh Phung Boulevard and Le Van Duyet Street. It seemed like a century had passed in the meantime. We'd aged with terrible swiftness, and, having lost all that we had lost, we were quite sure we did not want to lose a whole lot more.

This sentiment was far beyond an intellectual position. It was a primal need at a level rarely touched by political discourse which only those who have been very badly used can truly appreciate: we flinched at the thought that it might return and do all that to us again. That flinch became a significant fact of American political life and as such an item of some controversy, particularly during the administration of Ronald Reagan.

Reagan was still quite taken with the war, though he'd had nothing much to do with it except for dispatching the National Guard to briefly occupy Berkeley while he was governor of California, and he often referred to the heroism of the boys chasing Charlie out in the bush and the nobility of their purpose. His administration was also full of men who liked to say that what the country needed was a good war, get all this Vietnam stuff out of its system. Few of them had had much to do with the stuff they talked about, but that didn't slow their talk down. To them Vietnam was an extraordinary anchor to have to drag. Their eyes were full of Nicaragua and the avowedly Marxist government holding sway there since the overthrow of the dictator Somoza, a former ally of ours. It was the kind of place where we used to dispatch marines in a hot minute, especially if there were Reds involved, but now it was no secret even among Reagan and his men that the public simply would not tolerate such a dispatch.

So the administration began regularly to reference something they called the Vietnam syndrome. It was a kind of illness among the body politic, according to them. It was causing us to abandon our role as a superpower because we were not prepared to use our troops the way superpowers do. The syndrome itself was like a Pavlovian response. Whenever the issue of force came up, we thought about Vietnam. We had to put that behind us. Their obvious inference was that just because the last war had involved lying, bolstering oligarchs, thwarting ourselves and our own system of government, and pursuing self-defeat at every turn, it was sick to assume that every time the president needed to dispatch troops all that same stuff would start over again. We had to remember our higher purpose even if we had lost track of it in Vietnam. We still had interests to be defended, and we were letting the memory of the war obscure them. Remembering like we did was a kind of defeatism, an attack on the true American spirit of can-do enterprise and heroic preparedness. Buck up, there was no need to flinch.

Or so the Reagan men said.

Their argument gained a certain cachet and carried sway in some quarters, but never enough for the administration to openly use American troops in Nicaragua. Despite all his popularity, Ronald Reagan was simply unable to make that sale. So the president and his helpers, thwarted but not prepared to take no for an answer, proceeded to make the same war on the sly, using a collection of oligarchs and warlords for surrogates, lying about their activities to Congress, violating our democratic process, and spending lots of money to little military effect.

When all that was revealed, of course, a number of us flinched for all we were worth.

About the time all the talk of Vietnam syndrome was going on, a couple dozen men I knew from the old days held something of a reunion. The occasion was the twentieth anniversary of the first national draft card return, when some two thousand of us in eighteen cities around the United States had collected our draft cards and handed them over to the government with an announcement that we were in violation of the law and intended to stay that way. A number of the two dozen reunited Resistance alumni who ended up at my house for an afternoon barbecue had done time together at a prison camp in Arizona or a federal correctional institution along the Texas–New Mexico border or both.

It was a lot like any other kind of reunion. We were both familiar and unfamiliar to one another and talked about the old days, about people from the joint and what had happened to them, about wives, ex-wives, and children, about the sad stories some of our old friends had become. We still laughed over the time Dickie dumped a pile of three hundred draft cards at the feet of the San Francisco federal attorney and said he'd see him in court. We all cringed again at how crazy things had gotten by the time our organization had come apart and we all started serving our sentences.

Late that afternoon I ended up in my kitchen, leaning against the counter and talking with Joe. Joe's draft card had gone back with the others in that return whose anniversary we were celebrating, when he was a graduate student in the history department at UCLA. We'd ended up in maximum security together. Early in his sentence Joe decided he wasn't going to cooperate with the prison system, refused to work, and, as a consequence, did his entire sentence in lockup, confined to a five-by-nine cell except for an occasional walk down the hall to the shower. He did a lot of that time up on C Block, catty-corner from me. When I got back to my cell from work, he and I would talk through the bars about things we were reading. Joe trained as an auto mechanic after he got out and now repaired cars for a living. Around the time of our reunion, several national magazines had run stories by men our age who used their deferments to avoid conscription but now regretted having done so, and my conversation with Joe eventually drifted onto those stories.

One of the authors had even gone so far as to say that he wished he'd been drafted and sent to Vietnam because now, in middle age, he felt like he'd missed his generation's great adventure. I told Joe that it pissed me off to have someone talk that way now that all the dying was long done and all the prices had been paid. I called it Hollywood bullshit. Then I asked Joe what he thought.

Joe was perhaps the gentlest person I knew, and I had never heard him speak precipitously. Twenty years later he was no different. He rubbed his chin for a long while before commenting. "Well," Joe observed, "I guess he had his chance, didn't he?"

Those who had actually seized that opportunity and survived brought home whatever pain they had left over and mostly disappeared in the anonymity of civilian life. Some collected disability pensions; they were all eligible for all the benefits of the old GI Bill and guaranteed health care from the Veterans Administration for life. But there were no "Welcome Back" parades for any of these boys, no lingering in the spotlight, no victory celebrations. Few people wanted to hear the stories they had to tell, so few listened, and of course few talked. As a consequence, America at large had little sense of who this army returning from the war really was. And we have been tracking them from a distance ever since.

According to *The Washington Post*–ABC News poll conducted in early 1985 and published on the tenth anniversary of our war's end, 30 percent of American veterans who served in the Vietnam theater had gone on to attend some college, 43 percent now considered themselves middle class, 78 percent owned their own homes, 72 percent had voted in the 1984 presidential elections, and, of those, 70 percent had voted for Ronald Reagan. Fifty-six percent of all Vietnam veterans thought they had "personally benefited in the long run" from having been in the war, though only 48 percent of veterans of "heavy combat" felt the same way. Among those polled 87 percent thought we were justified in bombing North Vietnam, and 48 percent thought we were justified in destroying villages suspected of harboring Vietcong, while 9 percent had no opinion. Fifty-one percent thought our war had been the biggest event in their lives, 28 percent didn't want people to know they had been in the war, 77 percent still thought about all the dying they saw there, and 44 percent often dreamed they were back "in country," with the smell of heat and diesel fuel and buffalo dung and charcoal smoke and spent gunpowder all mixed up in the air, infantry rounds popping in the distance, howitzers registering somewhere close, and fear underfoot.

We have tracked the rest of our war's veterans from an even greater distance still.

Those who fought for the North Vietnamese Army or the National Liberation Front are known in Vietnam as *bo doi phuc vien,* "war veterans of the revolution." Though there are far more of them, and their experiences were generally much longer and more harrowing than our own, their visible incidence of severe post-traumatic stress disorder appears smaller. That is partly because it is hidden by an authoritarian political system, unwilling to admit its noble soldiers lie awake with nightmares and hallucinations, and partly because most of their veterans were volunteers in the first place, and they got their parade when it was over. Almost all of them receive military pensions. War invalids of the NVA and NLF are eligible for care for life, and the government offers financial incentives to women who marry them. Most live at home and are supported by their villages as well as the national government. *Bo doi phuc vien* also had priority for redistributed land in the years immediately following liberation, and, by the tenth anniversary of our war's end, some 70 percent of all posts in the Vietnamese provincial administration were filled by them.

Not surprisingly, the leftovers from the Army of the Republic of Vietnam, now known in their homeland as *linh nguy* or "puppet soldiers," have had it worst of all:

The restaurant was on a stretch of roadway on the far side of a village straddling two-lane Highway One, Vietnam's only continuous semimodern road. My guide, Tre, and his buddy, the driver, were a couple of Cholon cowboys who took great pride in their gourmet tastes and had a knack for finding great meals. This place was one of their best. We came upon it about halfway along the journey from Dalat to Nha Trang. We sat together at a rickety table on a concrete slab floor under a thatched roof with wide open sides. A hot breeze was drifting across the coastal plain. Our car, a six-year-old Toyota that played a Walt Disney tune whenever it was driven in reverse, was parked out back. All the restaurant's other rickety tables were full of Vietnamese, and the stereo system was playing Vietnamese rock and roll, cranked to top volume. It was hard even to hear each other when we talked, but the fried fish was fresh and done just right, as were the bean sprouts stir-fried with onion wedges and slices of tomato. We ate six courses, all for the equivalent of a little more than ten dollars American.

Even in the cacophony—with diners chattering, waiters easing around in flip-flops, dogs wandering in and out—the quiet, tiny figure, propped against one of the posts supporting the restaurant's roof watching all the eaters, was hard to miss. He was dressed in peasant shorts and the tattered uniform coat of an ARVN ranger, a unit that once had quite a reputation for ferocity. The ranger's coat sleeves were rolled up, revealing that one of them was almost vacant except for a gnarly stub far above where the elbow had once been. The pit of his good arm supported a homemade crutch. The leg on that side was nothing but stump as well. When the waiter brought our change and there was a pile of Vietnamese *dong* notes on the table, the ranger clumped up to within ten feet of us, motioned at himself, and held out his hand.

I asked Tre how much I should give him.

At the time, the *dong* was exchanging at 11,300 to the dollar. Tre pulled two one-hundred-*dong* notes out of the pile and waved them in the ranger's direction.

The ranger clumped over, took the money, and clumped back to his post without either making eye contact or saying a word.

I gulped my tea and told Tre and the driver it was time to get back on the road, *di di mau*.

When one goes looking for the war in today's Vietnam, it is not immediately obvious.

Sixty percent of the country is under the age of twenty-five, and when you ask a question about the war, they ask, "Which one?" The Vietnamese have fought two wars since ours, one a protracted occupation of Cambodia, the other a short and ferocious encounter with the Chinese along Vietnam's northern border. When I finally returned in 1995, capitalism was breaking out, and the arrival lounge at the old Tan Son Nhut Airport in the new Ho Chi Minh City reeked of money about to be made. Planeloads of Japanese and Korean businessmen were arriving daily.

The most constant reminders of the American War, now twenty years done, were the old deuce-and-a-half trucks, abandoned by the thousands when we departed from the embassy roof and still surviving by the dozens and dozens, hauling heavy things from here to there belching diesel and farting smoke. They were, however, mostly lost in the surrounding cacophony: motor-scooter horns, bicycle bells, tractor blats, Vespa whines, motorcycle backfires, old Peugeots coughing, new Toyotas humming, brake squeals, boom boxes with Vietnamese singing rock and roll, stereo Madonna whether you wanted it or not, creaking buses, whistles from pedicab drivers, and pidgin shouts about whatever was on the roadside for sale.

In fact, though it is hard to identify at first glance, I eventually learned the war had acquired a second life here in the present tense, this time as a venue for the booming tourism industry.

The civic attraction most frequently visited by foreign tourists in Ho Chi Minh City was the Exhibition House of Aggression War Crimes on Vo Van Tan Street in District 3, a twenty-minute pedicab ride from the Hotel Continental, where I was staying. The Exhibition House was a relatively small compound, ringed on two sides with a continuous concrete building that was divided into several exhibition rooms. The dirt courtyard featured a gift shop and a display of several captured American armored vehicles, artillery pieces, and a spotter plane. The gift shop sold mostly curios unrelated to the war, but it did have a selection of used Zippo cigarette lighters, left behind by the boys who departed in a hurry so long ago. The Zippos were inscribed with invocations of Tennessee, claims to be the Baddest Motherfucker in the Valley, odes to the Airborne, Thelma's initials, a verse from "The Eyes of Texas," the ace of spades, braggadocio about the First Marines and the Seabees, invocations of the Big Red One and the big red one, lists of places and dates like Cho San, June 1, An Khe, Mar. 29, names like Gunny, Bobo, and The Freak, recitations from the Marine Corps Hymn, and pleas for mercy in both English and Spanish. Some of the Zippos were well worn; others looked like some master sergeant had just now dropped them coming out of the PX.

The exhibitions at the Aggression War Crimes museum consisted almost entirely of old blown-up wire-service photos with crudely translated captions like "U.S. soldiers waiting outside people's shelter opening for arresting whoever getting out therefrom" or "U.S. soldiers killed then dragged along body remains after the raid." My disappointment was tangible, and I went to the museum office to vent it. The director was not in, so I spoke to his assistant, who recommended I write my comments in a book they reserved for that purpose, and I ended up doing that at length, penning a spontaneous appeal for them to devote serious resources to this subject. There was an enormous volume of material that could be explored in a genuine way by both sides of the war. This exhibit was entirely inadequate. Both sides needed to be shown what went on, but this showed nothing.

It took almost my entire pedicab ride back to the Continental with Vinh pedaling behind me in silence before I could get some perspective and laugh at the spectacle of me buttonholing the assistant director and him looking back at this gangling American as though he were dealing with someone missing more than a few slices out of his loaf.

I have since come to accept that exposure to the war's history and actual locations will be developed somewhat haphazardly here, in response to the market's demands. Already, the tunnels at Cu Chi, an infamous redoubt of the VC, have been redug for the inspection of tourists. At the site, several hours' drive outside Ho Chi Minh City, the adventuresome can fire an AK-47, just one dollar cash American per round. There are also several new tours along the DMZ, with stops at Camp Carroll, Khe Sanh, and the Rockpile.

In addition, the really enterprising tourists can find their way to Tu Du Hospital in Ho Chi Minh City.

There one of the medical specialties is ministering to those who were exposed to massive amounts of dioxin during the American program of chemical warfare and aerial defoliation that lasted almost half a decade. One ward is given over to young women who were breast-fed after their mothers were exposed. Those babies, grown and married, are now suffering an epidemic of cancers of the placenta during their own pregnancies. Another ward at Tu Du is given over to men from the same area admitted in uncommonly high numbers with liver cancers and cancers of the lung. There is yet another Tu Du ward for children born to parents with wartime dioxin exposure in their family trees. Most of these youngsters have bulging skulls, cleft palates, and stumps where they should have hands and feet. The hospital's laboratory also has preserved in glass jars a number of malformed fetuses with similar histories, even one with two heads.

Ho Chi Minh died before the war was over, and his legacy is at best bedraggled in Vietnam today. The country he founded is desperately poor, still coping with the damage from the fighting that ended twenty years ago, drained by its ten-year occupation of Cambodia, strangled by the twenty-year American embargo, and saddled with far less in the way of leadership than the promise of liberation once held. The hope and nationalism of the NLF have given way to a brand of

Communist rule that has provided neither reconcilia-
tion nor revival and after two decades of increasing
incompetency has degenerated into a system of entrenched privilege which, like its Chinese counterpart, has now tried to rescue itself by opening its
economic doors to outside investment.

One of the first signs of that opening was when
studying English, banned for eight years during the
1980s, was once again legalized. By the time I visited
Hue on the twentieth anniversary of the war's end,
our international capitalist language was everywhere.
Whenever I left my hotel, I was approached by students studying English at the nearby university and
looking for practice conversing. I was also approached
by others who were old hands at talking American and
on the lookout for a chance to keep their old hands in.

Freddie was one of the latter. He'd been an ARVN
interpreter attached to a unit of the American 101st
Airborne Division. He wanted to know if I needed a
guide for touring the Citadel or maybe some money
changed, real good rates. I said no on both counts, but
Freddie walked along with me for a bit anyway. When
we reached the Perfume River, just upstream from
where one of the city's bridges was finally being
repaired after the beating it took in 1968 when the
Americans recaptured Hue, Freddie offered me a
Winston. After I declined he lit one for himself off an
ancient Zippo. The gray morning was just breaking

up, revealing sunny patches the color of robins' eggs overhead, and, while I watched a small group of women with bare feet and bad teeth hauling baskets of sand for the bridge project, Freddie started going on about the old days, when the country was full of easy American money and his living was good.

So, I finally asked him, how's Communism been?

Freddie spat. "Communism sucks," he said. "Fuckin' number ten, you bet."

The American embassy in Saigon has stood vacant since the city fell to the advancing North Vietnamese and National Liberation Front armies at the end of April 1975. Its final hours were spent as the last embarkation point for an exodus of our old allies, many of whom are now living somewhere down the block and around the corner from the rest of us. Those final hours of departure were a travesty: the desperate bull rushing of the embassy gates, mobs of our Vietnamese, each waving notes from an American employer or a boyfriend or someone from Indiana who knew their uncle. They all came: our interpreters, the leaders of our surrogate army, our favorite barmen, the entire bureaucracy of the Republic of Vietnam, our stool pigeons, our loyal comrades, the ones we had used, the ones on whom we took pity, and the ones we owed a favor. Most had the crazed look of brokers who had sold short in a long market.

Travesty or not, our evacuation of those we did take was likely the noblest act we performed in all the dozens of rounds of enforced social engineering attempted during our ten-year stay in their homeland. Whatever the fix they might have been in if they were left behind, it was, more often than not, our fault they were in it. We were right to let them come, even the torturers of Miss Binh.

And come they did. The exodus lasted years and altered the face of America. People from Chu Lai now live in Massachusetts, people from Quang Tri live outside Chicago. Men who learned their trade on the South China Sea now fish the Gulf of Mexico. Both Orange County in Southern California and Santa Clara County in Northern California have drawn big enough concentrations of refugees to earn one of their neighborhoods the nickname Little Saigon. There are groceries that sell fermented fish sauce and restaurants that dish out noodle soup for breakfast, just like at home. There are video stores that feature low-budget martial arts movies knocked off in Hong Kong from scripts in which the son in the new world returns to the old to redeem his father's failure. These videos are a staple for the aimless young among them who have yet to find a place here. A network of gangs specializing in strong-arm robberies of homes and extortion of protection money has emerged on the edges of this exodus. At the same time, school districts all over California are now accustomed to valedictorians with names like Nguyen and Tai. There are Vietnamese playing Division I football and dancing with the bulls and bears on Wall Street. When appropriate their parents still fly the old Republic of Vietnam flag—three horizontal red stripes on a field of saffron. They have collectively made America a lot more different than it was before they came.

I doubt if any place has been changed more by this exodus than Fresno, California, my old hometown.

The agent of change in Fresno's case were the Hmong, a collection of loosely affiliated tribal groups that traditionally occupied the highland ridges of Vietnam and Laos along which ran the Ho Chi Minh Trail. During the war the Hmong were recruited by the CIA to threaten our enemy's logistics, with little success. The traditional Hmong life then was thatch houses, slash and burn subsistence agriculture, and a cash crop in opium poppies. More than 100,000 Hmong immigrated to America when the war was done, and, though the official policy was to disperse them widely, more have ended up in Fresno than anyplace else. They moved into the shoddy apartment complexes next to the muffler shops and taco stands, where all the rooms had glitter in the ceilings and were old before their time; they moved into the dying tract homes with broken Oldsmobiles in the driveways, and they moved into the decaying clapboards along the alleys in the old part of town where my grandma used to live.

At first they ate squirrels out of the park and planted opium in the vacant lots, but they learned. Now most want to get out of Fresno on the next bus. They are largely unemployed, some of their kids are trying to be gangsters, none of the young listen to the shaman anymore, and a lot don't even consult the elders. Most are on welfare, have been since they arrived, and, despite an endless round of mandatory job-search training classes and job-placement sessions, look likely to stay on welfare for the foreseeable future. During 1995 a number of the Fresno Hmong announced they weren't going to the worthless training sessions anymore, and the welfare department announced they would cut their welfare off if they didn't. That led to a demonstration by some 1,500 Hmong at Fresno's brand-new County Building. It eventually had to be broken up by a twenty-man police riot squad. The older among the Hmong, who still remembered the deal cut with the CIA, said they'd expected a lot more of America, but nobody except Hmong, and not all that many of them, were listening.

9

AMERICANS DON'T LIKE to lose, don't like losers, and had never lost a war before. But we lost this one. There are lots of explanations, but the simple truth is that we ran into a group of people who brought considerably more seriousness to this fight than we did: they lived underground, they huddled in the jungle, they moved by foot and bicycle, they fought on a little rice and a little ammunition. They absorbed enormous punishment, bore great sacrifice, endured untold hardship, and fought us and all our war machines to a dead stop. If they survived, they fought until the whole thing was done, some for as long as a decade. They did not back off, and they held the field until we finally lost our stomach for the fight and went home.

And not only did we lose, but we were poor losers. When we finally left, we left like a whipped dog, pissing on one last bush as we fled down the street.

During the second week of May 1975, the final American military action of the war was announced. I was at the Oakland Coliseum that evening, watching a National Basketball Association play-off game between the Chicago Bulls and the hometown Golden State Warriors. Saigon had fallen days earlier, and the sight of Americans fleeing off the embassy roof was still fresh in everyone's mind. During a break in the action, the Coliseum public-address system announced that the United States Marines, in response to the detention of the civilian cargo ship *Mayaguez* by the new Khmer Rouge government, had invaded an island off the Cambodian coast, fought a running gun battle with several Khmer Rouge units, freed the ship's crew, and evacuated. This final note was Gerald Ford's principal contribution to the history of our journey down the tunnel with no light at the end. In what would be recognized as the typical Ford fashion, the *Mayaguez* incident had a bumbling signature: the Khmer Rouge had released the ship's crew before the raid was under way. Thirty-eight marines died pointlessly in the ensuing action.

At the Oakland Coliseum that night, the initial announcement was accompanied by the illumination of a huge American flag on the far wall. The crowd, some fifteen thousand, already hyped by the game, leapt to their feet and celebrated this final outburst of American testosterone with a wave of wild applause, spurred on by the flashing scoreboard.

I kept my seat and hunched my shoulders against the noise, the rippling flag, the blinking lights. Few of the people cheering looked as though they had paid much of any price during the ten years that had preceded this final chest thumping, and the war was still a tender enough subject with me that I noticed such things. It had all been vicarious for them, all television and scorecards. I wondered if they would cheer so loudly if those thirty-eight wasted grunts had been dragged out on the court below, where they could get a good look at them, all mud and blood and time run out.

I had expected better, of course, but, like it or not, this was us. We went into the war blind to ourselves, and we left the same way.

The summer before last, I was driving south along U.S. 101 with my friend John, the Pacific on one side of the road and the best forests in California on the other. We were dirty and overgrown after a four-day backpack trip along the Smith River. My kids—one twenty-five years old, the other, twelve—were in my van's rear seat, asleep. John and I had organized together in the old days. Oregon and Washington were his turf, and I came in every couple of months to help out during the last year before I entered the custody of the attorney

general. John's a county public defense attorney now
and a better Buddhist than I. That day, almost three
decades later, we were talking about the war neither of
us could forget.

"I'll tell you where we lost our way," John said, looking out at the ocean, then turning to face me and
touching his hand to his chest. "We lost it in our
hearts."

I agreed. It was indeed all about heart.

When we needed ours, we could not find it and
could not care enough to stop ourselves, could not
value all we were about to lose, and, unable to value it,
we could not save it when the time came.

I remember. We lost so much more than any of us
ever imagined we would. We lost the legend of ourselves, we lost our heroism and our nobility, we lost all
perspective. We lost the string-bean kid third row left
in the third-grade photo, we lost the toes off a thousand
feet, we lost the place we once called home. We also
lost the allegiance of each of us to the other, the communion at the core of our national self. We lost our
right to pretend we were much different from the people we had once so routinely dismissed as venal tin-
horns and vicious thugs. We lost our innocence, our
standing, our reputation, our faith in who we were,
our dignity, the easy feeling when we looked at ourselves in the mirror. We lost the kid from down the
block, the kid from across town, the kid from up the

valley, the kid from over the creek, the kid from down by the bay, from up the state, from along the river, from downtown, from uptown, from the other side of the tracks, and from the very end of the road.

We lost in the long run, in the short run, and in every run in between. We lost coming and going, on this side and that. We lost the fantasies I once chased home after watching Roy Rogers down at the Tower Theatre and the illusions we all nurtured in the bowels of the chain of command. We lost much blood and more than a few tears. We lost legs from Dayton, spleens from Rochester, lungs from Boise, and kneecaps from Duluth. We lost billions and billions of dollars.

And we lost more sleep than we can remember, more joy than we can forget. We lost faith in our government, faith in each other, faith that anything was what it seemed. We lost our bearings, we lost our discipline, we lost our expectations of ourselves. We lost hope, we lost sight, we lost touch, we lost our good sense, our good name, and most every other good we had. We lost the knack for looking each other in the eye. We lost our clean conscience, and we lost track of who we were and who we weren't. We lost our capacity to tell real from unreal and true from false. We lost control and we never got it back.

We also lost track of the difference between right and wrong.

This is not easy for anyone to admit, but it is an especially uneasy enterprise for us. We are, after all, Americans. It never occurred to us that this war would transform us into a case history in moral dyslexia. Most of us figured we were bred right, born right, raised right, and didn't have to worry about that kind of thing anymore. I once did, and everybody I knew was the same way. We were Sunday school graduates, *Captain Kangaroo* alumni, the Duke's people, keepers of the White Hat and the eternal flame. We told ourselves that America always righted wrongs and never wronged rights.

As it turned out, we got little of it right and almost all of it wrong, and our war was the proof.

It was the wrong fight, at the wrong time, in the wrong place, against the wrong people, for the wrong reasons, with the wrong strategy, the wrong tactics, and the wrong weapons. It was the wrong approach, to the wrong situation, betraying the wrong motives, from the wrong perspective, with the wrong attitude, to the wrong end, using the wrong means, effecting the wrong result. It was both the wrong twist and the wrong turn, arriving inexorably, of course, at just the wrong moment. It was the wrong choice, the wrong answer to the wrong question, altogether the wrong way to take care of business. And it wronged just about everybody it touched: it wronged the wrong and it wronged the rest of us as well.

And now, twenty years after we finally left the war behind, all that hasn't changed. What remains is for us to finally engage in the public arithmetic and admit we had no right to have been there and no right to have done what we did and no right to continue pretending otherwise.

We all have our individual behaviors, for which we answer singly as well, in our dreams, if nowhere else.

Scott sat on one side of the steps, and I sat on the other. It was the middle of Florida, and, though the sun had fallen more than an hour before, it was August and the night lay like a pile of steaming laundry all over the porch. Scott had survived thirteen months in Vietnam with the Marine Corps, all of it out in the bush, mostly walking point at a time in the war when the average life expectancy of a marine point man was maybe three months. By the time his company joined the sweep of that coastal village he told me about, he was a sergeant and a self-confessed hard-nosed son of a bitch. That night on the porch, he was skinny and bearded, and his voice kept the same flat tone no matter what he talked about. Only his occasional laugh changed the timbre of his voice, but he wasn't laughing much that night.

On one side of the village, he said, he and his men took a few rounds from up the slope, but they never found who fired them. Then, on the other side, his men spotted an armed man in black pajamas scuttling down a hole and into a tunnel. The grunts clustered around the tunnel's mouth and called the sergeant. Shortly after Scott arrived, so did a young woman with hair that hung almost to her waist. She'd run out from a hut on the edge of the village. She started pleading in Vietnamese and threw herself across the opening behind which the man in black pajamas had disappeared.

The woman was crying and pleading and crying and pleading, and some of Scott's men started saying they ought to just cut it loose. Let the sucker live, man, the dude and the woman are in love. Fuckin' Romeo and Juliet, Sarge.

Scott told his men to get their shit together. The bitch and her boyfriend would just turn around and plunk one of them as soon as they turned their backs.

He grabbed the woman by her hair, wrapped it around a nearby sapling with a snap of his wrist, stepped back, and slammed several rounds from his M-16 into her forehead. She splattered all over the ground. Then he ordered grenades slung into the tunnel. The man in black pajamas was half jam when they finally pulled his body out.

Scott looked straight across at me, Florida dripping on his cheeks and his eyes narrow, a man comfortable in the dark. "I didn't give a fuck," he said. "I was gonna go home, and I didn't care who I had to kill to make that come true."

The frogs sounded from the lawn and the night steamed.

"Out where I was playin' the game, it was us or them, simple as shit. A fight's a fight."

If we ever pursue our reckoning, we will find that some locations concentrate our attention more than others. Porterville, California, is one of those.

Porterville, pop. 12,000 in 1968, may have lost more boys to the war per capita than anywhere in the United States. Of our 58,000 dead, 16 listed Porterville as their hometown, a total of 40 if you count the dead from several other even smaller towns around Porterville in that corner of the San Joaquin Valley: east of Highway 99, north of Bakersfield, edging up on the west slope of the towering Sierra Nevada. Porterville is an hour-and-a-half bus ride southeast of Fresno, through the cotton fields and the tomatoes and the peach orchards and alfalfa flats. My high school football team, nicknamed the Warriors, used to play theirs, nicknamed the Panthers. I remember their uniforms were orange and their fullback weighed more than anyone we suited up, but I don't remember much else. It was just another Valley town to me, out on the giant flat, fueled by the fields outside its city limits and marked by the Stars and Stripes flying in the park downtown. I was from the big city thereabouts, ten times the size of Porterville, where we had five high schools, several shopping centers, and a minor league baseball franchise, so Porterville didn't seem like all that much.

Of course, Porterville didn't pretend to be all that much either. It was a small town, pure and simple, where people worked and kids enlisted in the service when high school was over. Just about everybody in town knew at least one of the boys who died. They remember: those boys went off thinking they'd get it done and come back heroes, they had played war on the playground or in the open country all around town, and then they grew up and sent letters home from places like Khe Sanh, Da Nang, and Quang Nam province. A lot had daddies or uncles or cousins who had been in the marines or the infantry, fighting in places like Iwo Jima and Inchon. This latest generation of sons got drunk with their buddies before they went and flipped coins or consulted the Ouija board to see who would come back and who would not. Those who did not, returned home in aluminum boxes, their effects in a military-issue duffel bag and foot locker, with a letter from the Department of Defense explaining when it happened and how. One of those Porterville boys died on a land mine, another in front of a VC machine gun, another to a shell fragment from a mortar round, and yet another caught a slug on Mother's Day.

In Porterville, decades later, those poor boys are still missed.

The mother of one keeps her boy's bedroom just the way it was when he grew up.

The father of another keeps his son's final letter available to read: "I thank the Lord each morning I get up," his boy wrote on the last morning he ever got up. He didn't have a chance to mail his letter before being shot out on patrol, so it was in his pocket when he died. The envelope arrived at his dad's house with the boy's dried blood splatters on it.

Another mother remembered kissing her boy good-bye when he shipped out and saying this kiss would have to last for an awful long time. She had no idea just how long that would turn out to be.

The girlfriend of yet another dead boy remembered that he'd begged her to take his high school ring just before he left, but she said that he should keep it and give it to her when he came back.

That same boy's mother flew to Mexico City, visited the shrine of the Virgin of Guadalupe, and crawled on her hands and knees to beseech the Mother of Jesus to protect her son.

Another mother remembered that the man the army sent to tell her what had happened drove a pickup truck. When her boy's remains reached San Francisco, she received a telegram saying they had arrived but were "unviewable," so his mother never got to look at him one last time. It took a while for the box with what was left of her boy inside to reach Porterville, and when she called San Francisco to see what the holdup was, she was told there were "stacks and stacks" of bodies coming in and deliveries were a bit behind schedule.

Most of those in Porterville who remember the kids who disappeared forever still wonder about their end. They wonder if their homeboys suffered for long, if they saw it coming, if there was anyone with them, who they called out for in their death rattle. They wonder if there wasn't some small happenstance that could have made it all different. And that there wasn't and nothing could have is still hard to swallow.

When Porterville decided to erect a memorial to honor the boys it had lost, the town could have chosen any design it wished, but it passed on the more standard-brand approaches: Porterville commissioned no noble, crouching, marble infantrymen or valiant cast-bronze dog soldiers gazing into the distance. Instead, Porterville engraved a block of stone with their boys' names and erected a pole from which is suspended a war surplus Huey medevac chopper, with red crosses painted on its sides, a machine identical to the ones used to carry the wounded away for treatment. This one remains about twenty feet off the ground and seems to be swooping in for a mercy mission at a hot LZ.

That memory is now part of Porterville. And it perseveres the way things in Porterville do. The elementary school children visit the monument and their teachers read out the names; a vet who made it back comes by regularly and prays there with his rosary; sometimes the mothers come; lots of others drive by, some leave flowers.

And the Huey hovers and hovers and hovers, mute testimony to one small town's wish that someone might have rescued their poor lost boys before it was too late.

Porterville's Vietnamese counterpart is a hamlet outside the village of Son My in Quang Ngai province, labeled on old American maps as My Lai 4.

On March 16, 1968, Charlie Company, First Battalion, Twentieth Infantry Regiment, Eleventh Brigade, Americal Division, United States Army, paid this part of the Quang Ngai countryside a visit. The area around Son My was dotted with hamlets referred to among the Americal Division as Pinkville because the whole bunch were considered VC territory. The Tet Offensive was just done, our army was still smarting from the humiliation, and now it was obvious that our enemies moved anywhere they wanted outside the major cities and, after dark, controlled most of the countryside. Our strategy of the moment was to root out their nests, and Pinkville certainly qualified as one of those. So the Americal boys loaded up on choppers at first light, and Charlie Company was dispatched to My Lai 4. An artillery barrage preceded them. The villagers were familiar with such bombardments, and every family had long since dug an improvised shelter to which they now retreated. When they emerged, they heard the chopper sounds. Like all American units, this one arrived in a clatter.

For Charlie Company, Pinkville was a cold LZ. In fact, through their entire visit to My Lai, they received no hostile fire at all. Charlie Company did not even encounter more than two or three men of military age, and the company's only casualty was a soldier who shot himself in the foot. The principal NLF cadre for the hamlet, who would have organized any opposition, had gone to a bunker three hundred yards from the village at the first sound of helicopters and stayed there throughout what followed.

Charlie Company's three platoons advanced from the LZ, arranged with the First and Second platoons across the front and the Third Platoon and company command bringing up the rear. Their orders were to sweep through My Lai and the surrounding area. The people they found were old men, women, and children, and when First Platoon approached the hamlet proper, its occupants did not run. They knew the Americans assumed anybody who ran was a VC and shot them, so everybody stayed put. Our boys then began rounding people up in the central plaza. There were no physical protests, though some repeated out loud "No VC, no VC."

The killing started when one of the First Platoon pushed an old man and then stabbed him in the back with his bayonet. When the man fell to the ground, the soldier finished him off with a bullet to the head. Then the same soldier picked up another fifty-year-old man, dropped him down a well, and threw a live M-26 grenade in on top of him.

The rest, of course, is history. Some twenty women villagers were clustered next to a rude temple where joss sticks were burning. The boys of Charlie Company executed all of the women with M-16 rounds to their heads. Soon M-16s were popping all over the hamlet. The lieutenant commanding First Platoon left the group guarding the villagers in the plaza with the instructions "You know what I want you to do with them," and when he returned and found the situation unchanged, the lieutenant made it explicit and said, "I want them dead." His troops stood some fifteen feet from the huddling villagers, including infants and grandmothers. The mothers tried to shield their children, but our troops shot every last one. The captain commanding Charlie Company arrived while it was happening and just watched.

Meanwhile, his Second Platoon was systematically sweeping ahead, destroying livestock and crops and firing their weapons into all the huts they came upon. By then, of course, villagers were running every which way, trying to escape. Second Platoon radioed the company commander with a report, and the company commander said to get on with it. Third Platoon was the last to reach My Lai proper and found bodies all over when they arrived. Third Platoon also added to the total. Several groups of fleeing villagers were chopped up by fire from the helicopter gunships circling overhead, and one large fleeing cluster ran straight into Third Platoon, who blew away as many as they could before the villagers scurried back the other way and out of sight.

Charlie Company was now running totally amok. Several enlisted men clicked their M-16s onto rock and roll and shot a woman until chips of her bones flew in the air. Another found an eight-year-old and his younger brother. The eight-year-old tried to cover the other's body with his own, but the soldier shot them both. An old woman was executed point-blank with an M-79 grenade launcher. Another member of Charlie Company shot a young woman with a baby and, when she fell, walked up and finished off the infant. A half dozen others swept through a field, found a wounded girl, and finished her off with automatic weapon fire. Several would later say they saw the company commander do likewise. Throughout the hamlet, soldiers from Charlie Company ordered the residents into the bunkers in which they'd taken refuge from the artillery earlier in the morning, and when each bunker was full, the soldiers threw in live grenades and slammed the hatch.

The last and largest group of villagers was rounded up next to a dry ditch. The lieutenant from First Platoon ordered the villagers shoved into the ditch and then ordered his troopers to waste everybody in it. The villagers begged, pleaded, cried, screamed, offered themselves, and tried to cover their babies. A half dozen of the Americans cut loose with their rifles and grenades anyway. One hundred and seventy bodies were later found there. When our soldiers were done, just standing by the ditch, a two-year-old child who had somehow survived all the firing emerged out of the pile of bodies and began stumbling back toward the hamlet. The lieutenant commanding the First Platoon chased the bawling toddler, picked him up, threw him back in the ditch, and shot him.

Charlie Company, First Battalion, Twentieth Infantry, finished its visit to My Lai 4 by burning all the hootches and exploding the hamlet's few brick structures. The company took a break afterward, time enough to lay out in the grass and have a smoke. It was barely noon, and the boys from the American Division had just finished killing 504 people. Some of the soldiers pulled out K rations and ate a quick lunch.

All of the My Lai dead were reported up the chain of command as VC killed in action, and Charlie Company's report made such an impact on the March 16 body count that General William Westmoreland, commander of all our forces in Vietnam, sent the company a personal message congratulating them on their "outstanding action."

Less than a year later, when news of the massacre leaked into the press, the army investigated everyone involved and, despite a finding by the investigating general that a whole litany of war crimes had been committed by officers and enlisted men, the army declined to bring charges against anyone except the lieutenant from the First Platoon. He was convicted of thirty-three counts of murder and sentenced to a dishonorable discharge and life in prison. That sentence was reduced by Richard Nixon to twenty years, then further reduced with a presidential parole bestowed not long before Nixon himself resigned in dishonor. The lieutenant from the First Platoon was imprisoned a total of some three years, much of it simply confined to officers' quarters at a Georgia army base. Then he went home to work in his father-in-law's jewelry store.

The hamlet his men decimated was rebuilt several years after the war ended and resettled mostly by immigrants from other parts of Pinkville and the surrounding province, organized into an agricultural cooperative. The settlers created a small museum featuring pictures of all the dead women and children and photos of American soldiers clipped out of magazines. They also put up a statue and a plaque with all 504 names inscribed on it.

Not long after the twenty-fifth anniversary of Charlie Company's descent into My Lai 4, I was surfing television channels late at night, unable to sleep for all the emptiness death had brought to my own house, when I stumbled across an interview with one of the few My Lai residents who survived that March 16 infantry sweep. She was sitting in front of the plaque of names and wailing between sentences. She also broke regularly into sobs. She had been in the ditch and survived because she was small and was covered up with the bodies of others. Her mother and father, brother and sisters had all been executed. She said she would never forgive the Americans for what they had done.

The Americans are us, of course, but I, for one, didn't blame her, I didn't blame her at all.

There has been no escaping the war for me.

It meant far too much, and I was in far too deep to just let it drop, so it has lingered nearby for the twenty-odd years since the last American caught the last chopper out of Saigon: lingered largely unaddressed, on the horizon one day, on my chest the next, a war that is over but nowhere near done.

I still cannot listen to the whump of helicopter rotors without recalling now middle-aged evening news footage of American boys, armed to the teeth, arrogant and terrified, leaping through the downdraft and into the tall grass, ten thousand miles from home.

Most came back, many came back in pieces, and some didn't come back at all. I remember, and, like many who lived through the war, I remain suspicious of power and have never regained much respect for the exercise of force. I still have little use for patriotic displays and no use at all for military conscription. I close my eyes and see wire-service photos of peasants in black pajamas huddling together in the hope of simply making it through the afternoon without being shot or burned alive, and I am still haunted by how easily we defiled and abused, devoid of reflection, hidden from ourselves by a veneer of geopolitics and a parking lot full of denial. I still assume deceit and hypocrisy whenever politicians start dispatching youngsters around the world to kill and be killed. Most of the boys I grew up with learned that lesson the hard way. Leaders eager to talk the talk did their best to send us to the far side of the Pacific when it came time to walk the walk, and there things turned a lot uglier and a lot more evil than we ever imagined. Our America debased itself out in that tall grass ten thousand miles from home, sowing pain over all hell and gone for no good reason, no good reason at all.

It was wrong, and nothing has been quite right for us since.

ABOUT THE AUTHOR

DAVID HARRIS was born and raised in Fresno, California, where he was named Fresno High School Boy of the Year in 1963. He attended Stanford University and was elected student body president in 1966. During his undergraduate years, he was active in the civil rights movement in Mississippi and gained recognition as a national leader of the opposition to the Vietnam War. In 1968, he resisted the draft, and upon his conviction for violating the Selective Service Act, he was forced to leave his pregnant wife, the folksinger Joan Baez, to spend nearly two years in federal prisons. Three months after his release, he and Joan Baez separated and began divorce proceedings. After the Paris Peace Agreements were signed in 1973, Harris began a career in journalism which, with the exception of standing as the Democratic party's unsuccessful nomination for Congress in California's Twelfth Congressional District in 1976, he has pursued ever since. In 1977, Harris married Lacey Fosburgh, a novelist and reporter for *The New York Times*. In 1993, Fosburgh died of breast cancer. The author of six previous books, including *Dreams Die Hard* and *The Last Stand*, Harris lives in Mill Valley with his son, Gabriel, and daughter, Sophie.